LAUREL

EVERYONE'S BEST FRIEND.

BY

STEVE MOORE

Note for Librarians: a cataloguing record for this book that includes Dewey Classification and US Library of Congress numbers is available from the National Library of Canada. The complete cataloguing record can be obtained from the National Library's online database at:
www.nlc-bnc.ca/amicus/index-e.html
ISBN 1-4120-2621-0

TRAFFORD

This book was published on-demand in cooperation with Trafford Publishing.
On-demand publishing is a unique process and service of making a book available for retail sale to the public taking advantage of on-demand manufacturing and Internet marketing. On-demand publishing includes promotions, retail sales, manufacturing, order fulfilment, accounting and collecting royalties on behalf of the author.

Suite 6E, 2333 Government St., Victoria, B.C. V8T 4P4, CANADA
Phone 250-383-6864   Toll-free 1-888-232-4444 (Canada & US)
Fax 250-383-6804   E-mail sales@trafford.com   Web site www.trafford.com
TRAFFORD PUBLISHING IS A DIVISION OF TRAFFORD HOLDINGS LTD
Trafford Catalogue #04-0449   www.trafford.com/robots/04-0449.html

13   12   11   10   9   8   7   6   5   4   3   2   1

This book is dedicated to my Parents Diana and Roy Moore for their love, kindness and belief in everything I do.
To my wonderful partner, Christine for her love and understanding. To my dear ol' friend Peggy, who has been my friend for many years and of course to the best friend I'll ever have – Laurel.

Bless you all.

Steve

INDEX

Chapter One.................................Decision Time.

ChapterTwo......."Six Staffordshire Bull Terriers For
                                                sale"

Chapter Three.............................Coming Home.

Chapter Four...................Early Days (And Nights).

Chapter Five.....................First Visit To The Vets.

Chapter Six...Training.

Chapter Seven..................................The Storm.

Chapter Eight......................Another Big Decision.

Chapter Nine.....................................Letting Go.

Chapter Ten...................................Laurel's Field.

Chapter Eleven...........................Operation Time.

Chapter Twelve...................................Jealousy.

Chapter Fourteen........................My Dear Ol' Nan.

Chapter Fifteen.............................Earlham Park.

Chapter Sixteen.............Moving House And Home.

Chapter Seventeen..................................Dave.

Chapter Eighteen.................Behavioural Problems.

Chapter Nineteen...........................Starting Over.

Chapter Twenty.....................................P.A.C.T.

Chapter Twenty One..........New Home, New Family.

Chapter Twenty Two................Funny Little Ways.

Chapter Twenty Three...................A Sad Discovery.

Chapter Twenty Four......."Devil Dog Savages Child"

Chapter Twenty Five...................The Present Day.

Author's Comments.............The Correct Decision?

FOREWARD

I am often asked the question "why do I care for animals so much?" The answer is simple. Most animals can't care for themselves. They can't tell you what the problem is. When any animal attacks it's for a reason, maybe fear, food or protection of it's young, but all we see is the devastating effect after the attack. There are only a very few animal species (humans being one of them) that will attack for no reason. The animals are incapable of informing us humans of their own fears. The only way they know how is to attack through instinct, probably after giving warning signs that we; ourselves have not bothered to look for.

The mountain gorillas in Rwanda are now almost extinct because of their trust in man. It's all a vicious circle. They are guarded by the decent people in Africa and have learnt to trust their "keepers" but unfortunately cannot distinguish between the guards and the poachers. It's because of their trust in humans that poachers are able to get so close to their prey and it's because of us humans who buy such disgusting souvenirs that the poachers are there in the first place. A true case of supply and demand. Without the sick need for tacky animal souvenirs and the rich man wanting a baby gorilla or monkey for a pet there would be no need for poaching. The poachers are not solely to blame.

The mountain gorilla is not unique in this, it's happening to all species in some form or another and I feel the need to do what I can to try to stop it, even if it's only to make other people aware of what is going on.

Animals need all the help they can get from the domestic animals like our own to the wild animals in Africa and I intend to carry on doing what I can for them as long as I am able. Maybe sometimes it does affect me in ways that it shouldn't but that is the way I am. I have shed many tears for the cruelty of the animals on this earth but I now have to tell myself the only way I can help them is to be strong and do what I can to help prevent these terrible things from happening. I just wish a few more people thought as I do. As I always say "I'm not an animal rights campaigner, just someone who cares for animals".

The writing of this book has nothing to do with the wild animals of this planet but a "simple" domestic dog. My dog Laurel who has been my constant companion for the last seven years inspired it's writing. What began as more of a diary for myself than anything else turned into something I realised other people, especially other dog 'owners' maybe interested in. I also hope this book will allay some of the public bad feeling towards bull terriers in general and promote the fact that they are not the "macho" dogs to 'own'.

Some of the stories are very funny, some are extremely sad but I have been totally honest and frank and all the stories are all true. It's never very pleasant re – living sad times but I am lucky to be able to say that the good times by far out-weigh the bad. I hope you enjoy reading this book as much as I have enjoyed writing about this truly remarkable dog.

STEVE MOORE

CHAPTER ONE

DECISION TIME

About ten years ago shortly after my little cat Harriet (Harri as she's known) came to stay I seriously started considering owning a dog. I was given Harri by a friend of mine on 5th April 1992 shortly after my granddad died. It was a total spur of the moment episode after I had just watched Norwich City beaten in the semi final of the F.A. Cup against Sunderland at my works social club. I'd had several beers and my friend Leslie Edwards asked if I wanted a cat as her brother had several kittens going begging. Not in the literal sense of course. Always being the great animal lover I said yes, even though being slightly the worse for wear from alcohol, I wondered if it was such a good idea. It was obvious Leslie knew the type of person I was because she has said on numerous occasions she knew I wouldn't change my mind and off load the cat even when I did sober up.

Within half an hour Leslie returned from her brothers closely followed by her daughter Helen with a tiny ball of fluff – that ball of fluff soon became known as Harriet (my favourite girls name by the way) This was the beginning of a long and sometimes fiery relationship.

She has certainly mellowed with years and now she greets me every time I arrive home from work or even if I just venture out into the garden. The one thing I frequently say about Harri is, "she's always there". Whenever I call her and she doesn't appear I become concerned, even though I know she ventures little further than her own garden.

It hasn't always been that way with Harri and me. Probably caused through my natural tormenting streak she was quite a vicious little cat at times although now, at eleven years old she is very loving and "people friendly". She will always jump on your lap for a cuddle, purring madly, which can be very therapeutic for us humans.

After being put off from having a dog by friends and family it wasn't till the middle of 1996 that I started considering it again. To be fair, I do tend to agree. 1992 probably wasn't the right time for me to buy a dog as I was still quite young and loved my all night parties! Cats can be left as long as there is food and water available but not so with our canine friends.

The thought of owning a dog really appealed to me in early 1997 as at that time, six years ago I was living alone – apart from Harri, that is. I was seeing somebody at the time but I didn't honestly think that relationship was going to last – something I was later proved right on. I have always loved animals and always had a real love for dogs. We had a couple of dogs as children as did my grandparents – in fact they once owned a Staffordshire Bull Terrier called Tiger (a very apt name as it turned out) Myself though, I had never actually owned a dog of my own so I began thinking seriously about the prospect of sharing my home with another four legged friend. I don't like using the word "owning" because it sounds very subservient and I do feel both animals have given me far more happiness than I could ever wish to give them. In the literal sense, yes, I do own them but in the moral sense we own each other.

The first thing I had to consider was what breed of dog I was interested in. That question was easily answered when I first met my son Steven's dog Arnie for the first time. Arnie was a rescued Staffordshire bull terrier or "Staffie" as they are sometimes refereed to. He was very big and tremendously solid but had no aggressive tendencies what so ever, even to me, a complete stranger. He had obviously been ill treated with previous owners because as soon as I picked up a newspaper to read he cowered in a corner of the room – such a pitiful sight. The only real contact with dogs I had had up till then was with my good friends Graham and Margaret's Boxer dogs, Holly and Lily who always loved the rough and tumble approach. On one occasion I tried this with Arnie, slapping him on his rump (something I always did with Holly) but to my amazement poor Arnie cowered to the floor. When I looked over to Steve he said, "He thinks he's done something wrong". Needless to say I went straight to him to reassure him and also made sure there was no repeat of this incident with Arnie. Arnie was such a wonderful dog and I have very fond memories of him. Unfortunately they are just memories as he passed away a couple of years ago, much to the sadness of Steven and myself. One image I have of Arnie is when Steve tied his "tugger" to the tree in his back garden. Having got Arnie interested, Steven walked away leaving Arnie hanging about a foot off the floor, growling madly, with no intention of letting his "tugger" go.

Steven also told me the story of when he would get up during the night to use the toilet, on returning to bed he would find Arnie in there refusing to move. Rather than

13

disturb him, Steve would pull a quilt and pillow on to the floor and go back to sleep. Just one of the characters I think my son has inherited from his father.

When I visited Steven's house in Wickford, Essex, it was only to bring him back to my house for a holiday and after a while I think Arnie realised this, as he never seemed that pleased to see me. I think he realised that whenever I turned up Steven would disappear for a few days, something he really didn't like. On one occasion when I actually took Steven home we arrived to find Arnie in a very sorry state. I was really concerned as he was lifeless. He also looked very sad (I honestly think "staffies" can put on a sad face if they want to). I said my goodbyes and left telling Steven if he didn't improve he should consider telephoning the vet. I need not have worried because apparently I had not reached second gear in the car before Arnie was running around the garden like a lunatic, so happy to have his best friend home. We can only assume he thought as I was in the house I would be taking Steven away again and wanted to make his protests known. What a dog!

Having decided it had to be a Staffordshire bull terrier I then started to do a little research into the breed. I read books and spoke to owners and I must say all was positive. The one problem I did have was Harri. I was, however, convinced that if our new addition was brought into the house in the correct way they could actually grow up together. I would also always be there to supervise when they were together should any problems occur.

I have to be honest and say I think I would have had a dog sooner had I not been put off by a number of family and friends.

14

Here are some of their statements:
    "It'll ruin your house"
    "They are a tremendous tie"
    "Vicious animals always biting people"
    " It'll probably kill Harri"
    " You're only buying a broken heart"

The last one I can probably agree with but as for the rest, in my humble opinion, they are all down to the owners (I've just used that word again). Having a well-trained animal is easy with patience and is so rewarding to both animal and carer (that's a better term). I will admit to not being the most patient of people as far as every day life goes but with animals it's never ending – something I think they fully deserve.

Before even thinking about having a dog I had a long chat with my then girlfriend Teresa about my work pattern. I had decided that, although I wanted my dog able to be left for short periods without causing problems I still had to work my 12 hour shift pattern (two 12 hour days and two 12 hour nights) and it would be impossible to leave a very young puppy for that length of time. As Teresa only worked part-time it was decided that on my working shifts she would stay to look after her. I certainly would not have gone ahead if this were not possible.

I had now made my mind up as to which breed I wanted so it was now the wait until the right one came along – I didn't have to wait too long.

CHAPTER TWO.

"SIX STAFFORDSHIRE BULL TERRIERS FOR SALE"

The advertisement in our local Evening News wasn't long in coming. I would estimate a couple of weeks at most. The thing that really caught my eye was how it was worded.

> *"SIX STAFFORDSHIRE BULL TERRIER*
> *PUPPIES FOR SALE. EXCELLENT*
> *TEMPERAMENT. MUM, DAD AND*
> *GRANDMUM CAN BE SEEN £250."*

The mere fact that the parents could be seen really meant something to me, as chances are that if the parents have a good temperament then you have a head start with the pup. Of course this doesn't always follow because as I have said before, the carer is the most important factor in the relationship. Any animal will only be as good as it's carer lets it be. I had made a couple of golden rules for myself prior to the visit to see the puppies. I knew they were all going to be cuddly little animals and all would look wonderfully attractive to me – the worlds number one animal lover – so I decided that I was not going to "fall in love" with the first ones I saw but keep my sensible head on and not make any rash decisions (easier said than done). I wanted to make sure I chose the right one. Also I had decided I wanted a male not a female (thinking of the brown patches on my lawn – petty, I know, but I do like a nice green lawn). These two rules I was definitely going to stick to.

17

One evening in early February 1997 I took a drive out to nearby Tacolneston in Norfolk to have a look at the puppies – the ones I was not going to "fall in love" with. Upon arrival I was lead towards the kitchen and on opening the door a sight was bestowed upon me that I will never forget. There in a fairly large plastic dog bed were 6 of the loveliest staffy puppies I had ever seen – I had fallen in love. With no grown up dogs in sight I went down to greet them, at that time not realising they were only 4 weeks old. They were all whimpering and falling around in the bed, rolling on one another and even chomping at each other's ears. It truly was a lovely sight. All were jet black apart from one who was brindle and white so you can imagine this one did stand out a little. One of the black pups came over to me and started making puppy-growling noises, which I found highly amusing. I thought I'd have a bit of fun with him so I pushed him over onto the soft bedding and said " come back in a couple of years and you may stand a chance" much to everyone's amusement. I hope he's forgotten that remark because if he did turn up now I think he would stand more than just a chance! After sitting on the floor with the pups for a while I began asking various questions and talking with the owners. It was then the little brindle and white female pup clambered out of the bed and made her way over to me. Ignoring everyone else she approached me whimpering like a child and I honestly believe she was asking me to choose her. I picked up and cuddled her for quite sometime while she almost fell asleep in my arms. I had almost made up my mind – that's both golden rules out of the window. All I wanted to see now was the parents if only to gauge their temperament. The father to the puppies lived at Newton Flotman, near Norwich and had the wonderful name of Atta Boy. I also found out that their great great grand dad on their

18

fathers side was a champion named Fulfin Black Eagle and great great granddad on mum's side was also a champion called Pitmax The Matador (wonderful names). I discovered that it was mum and grand mum that lived with the pups but it would be no problem to visit dad as long as I made arrangements to do so. I decided mum and grand mum would suffice. After being pre-warned that although both dogs were boisterous they were not aggressive, they were let in. Both dogs came bounding in, all over me licking my face, pushing my legs and generally doing anything possible to get my attention – something they already had 100%. It felt like I had known them for years or I was a long lost friend returning home after being away for months. Grand mums name was Queenie and mums name was Gemma Crazy Lady (an extremely apt name) and both dogs had excellent temperament (although crazy) just as the advert in the newspaper had said. Gemma was exactly the same build as my dog is today and although very solid, not as big as grand mum. Seeing these two had made my mind up – I wanted the little brindle and white female or should I say she wanted me. It's always said you don't choose a dog, it chooses you and that in this case was very true. Mum jumped into her bed with the little ones immediately being swamped for food. I asked the owners if I could hold "my" dog one more time and was assured that Gemma wouldn't mind in the slightest. This would be the real test, I thought. I gingerly crouched down and put my hand in the basket to pick up "my" dog. Gemma sniffed and licked my hands, frantically wagging her tail while grand mum looked on. No problems at all. Now I knew I had made the right choice. I left a deposit, kissed "my" dog goodbye and promised to return in a week to bring her to her new home.

I left the house knowing I had made the right choice but I also knew there was some hard work to be done in training and also preparing my home for a new arrival. I must admit that night I was a very happy man.

CHAPTER THREE

COMING HOME.

Now, as far as I was concerned there was no turning back. I had made the commitment and there was no way I was going to back out. I now had a week to prepare the house for my little dog to come home to.

The first thing I had to buy was somewhere for her to sleep so I bought a full size dog bed. I knew she would be lost in it initially but with quilts and covers I would make it snug and warm and after all she would grow into it wouldn't she? I made sure she had her own food and water bowl and plenty of toys to keep her occupied. Most animals only start destroying the furniture through boredom so toys were a priority.

The next thing I had to do was to think of a name for her. The one thing I didn't want to do was give her a "macho" name that would not suit. I was never going to encourage her to be a bully or to be aggressive, although it's pretty difficult to stop the bullying instincts of a Staffie. I really wanted to name her after one of my heroes but that was where the problems started. Aside from my parents, my heroes are Muhammad Ali, Stan Laurel and Oliver Hardy. Let's just take a look at those names. Muhammad was, I think you have to agree, a definite no, no. Ali - yes it's got a ring to it. Stan – not really for a little girl. Oliver – no. I was seriously thinking of Olly at the time but my friends Graham and Margaret had just bought another Boxer and called her Holly so it was a bit to close. Hardy – no. Really that only left Laurel. The more I said it the more I liked it. It was a girls name and it didn't portray a "macho" dog like "Tyson", "Satan" or "Brutus". My vet once said to me he would feel a bit easier if a dog came in with a name like "Laurel" to a dog with a name like "Satan". Only a name but it's some indication of how the carer perceives its dog. With her name decided I then had a week to look forward to her coming home.

Exactly one week later almost to the hour I was back on the road to Tacolnston to fetch Laurel home. I remember the night so vividly – it was in mid February, very cold and slightly foggy. A real "pea – souper" wouldn't have stopped me bringing her home that night. When I arrived we went through almost the same ritual as the previous week. This time, however I made a big fuss of Queenie and Gemma first. I felt so guilty that I was coming to take one of her babies away so she had an extra special fuss. Still mad, still boisterous but still wonderful dogs. I went into the kitchen again to see the pups and to see my Laurel (who was fast asleep at the time). I was assured that all the pups had been weaned from mum but I was unaware until I later looked at the date of birth (6.6.97) that they were only five weeks old. Some of the blame for this must be down to me, as I should have checked. I certainly would not have brought her away from her mum that early had I have known.

Having sorted the paperwork, the pedigree and the finances I placed Laurel, still asleep, in a small blanket inside small plastic container that I had brought along specially. She must have been only seven or eight inches long and looked so helpless. I felt almost as bad for taking her from her mum, Gemma as I did for Gemma losing her little one. Gemma, however still had five pups to care for and Queenie around. Laurel only had me. As I left to place Laurel in the car the young daughter in the family sobbed. Laurel was her favourite pup. I made her a solemn promise that I would love and care for Laurel and make her a dog to be proud of – something, hopefully I am still fulfilling to this day.

I drove home to my house at Old Catton in Norwich exceptionally carefully that night, not just because of the fog but also because of my little passenger. She whimpered for some of the journey, obviously frightened that all her brothers and sisters had disappeared and mum and grand mum weren't around either. After all, it was all she had been used to the past few weeks. The guilt came over me again. I was desperately hoping Harri would "adopt" her, at least that way she would have another four-legged friend to comfort her.

CHAPTER FOUR

EARLY DAYS (AND NIGHTS)

When we arrived home I took Laurel straight into the kitchen, talking and reassuring her all the time. Harri was downstairs in a flash, obviously either smelling or sensing something strange. Having placed Laurel, still in her little tray, on the floor, I watched with care to see how the first meeting between Harri and Laurel would pan out. As I suspected, there was no need for concern. Harri, being about three times the size of Laurel was showing no fear or aggression towards her whatsoever and at the age Laurel was I don't think she knew what either of those feelings were. Harri slowly wandered around sniffing while all Laurel could do was to give a little whimper. I then decided to let Laurel free to have a wander but as soon as I placed her on the kitchen carpet she stuck to it like Velcro. Her tiny little nails were like pins and she just couldn't prise then from the carpet. My first call to Graham and Margaret for some dog advice was not long in coming – ten minutes after getting her home – not bad. After Margaret had made a call to our friend Carol and then called me back on how to cut, how far to cut and where to cut the nails I gave them a little trim so at least the poor mite could walk around on the carpet. Her first venture into the lounge resulted in a small wet patch about the size of a fifty pence piece being left in the middle of the floor. I immediately picked her up and put her on some newspaper (her first training session had begun). I can honestly say it is one of the few times she ever did that on the floor, not through scolding when she

25

did wrong but through praise when she got it right. I spent most of that evening with her asleep on my lap. I felt just as contented as she looked.

When it came to bed time I made a fatal mistake, (or so I was told by the vet on our first visit) I felt so guilty about Laurel being on her own I decided to take her bed in my room and let her sleep there for the night. I had no intention of keeping up this practice but just for the first couple of nights until she got used to the fact that she only had me.   Before going to bed that night I placed Laurel's extremely large dog bed at the foot of my own bed. In it was a large soft quilt, a hot (or should I say warm) water bottle, a few toys and a ticking clock. I had read that the warmth of the bottle and the ticking of the clock could emulate the puppies' mother – the clock replacing her heartbeat. Whether all of these things actually help or not, I don't know but I'm sure it gave her some comfort after leaving her family behind. I also placed newspaper beside her bed just in case and a bowl of water. As soon as I placed her in her bed she gave a little whimper and she was soon fast asleep, even though I wasn't! I stayed awake for best
part of that night until utter exhaustion took over and I slept.

I was awoken by the whimper I had now got used to and the constant licking of her lips. Was she thirsty and didn't know where the water bowl was? It was the first night after all. I got up to check. I actually had to wet her mouth with the water before she would take some but I did eventually work and she settled down again. It wasn't too long before I was woken up again, this time by my little friend whimpering beside my bed. She had clambered out of her own bed and stood beside me trying to get my attention, which she duly got. I picked her up (another fatal mistake) and laid her on my chest. She loved the warmth and closeness almost as much as me. Within minutes she was snoring so, like a child I decided to place her back in her own bed. When I picked her up she was like a rag doll, head and legs lolling all over but asleep. I laid her in her own bed and tried to get more sleep myself. There was little package and a small wet patch left right next to the newspaper I had laid but it was close enough for me to know she had, at least tried to reach it.

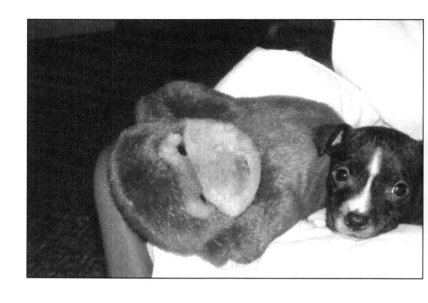

One of the first pictures taken of Laurel. She's the one on the right!

By the time it was morning, needless to say I was shattered. Laurel was fine; she could sleep all day if she wished. I did say if *she* wished. When I took her downstairs into the kitchen it was time to explore all over again. Both Harri and her having a good smell of each other wandering round into different rooms and even trying to climb the stairs. Harri was I little weary of Laurel although not too threatened because of her small size. Laurel, on the other hand was showing absolutely no fear of Harri whatsoever, even attempting to chase her at times, albeit very slowly. I'm not sure if she was playing or wanted mothering.

Our first day together was quite funny really. After giving Laurel her breakfast of a little scrambled egg (wrong move according to the vet) she began following me everywhere. This was probably just for comfort on her part although it did feel nice for me. I laid her quilt on the kitchen floor where she duly climbed into and went to sleep. I felt that tired I could have so easily joined her but I thought I would make the best of the quiet period and do whatever jobs I had to do.

I telephoned the vet to make an appointment for Laurel to be checked over. It sounds funny saying this now but I had an immense feeling of pride for Laurel, maybe because she was the first dog I had ever really had but it did feel right. The rest of the day was spent playing cuddling and sleeping. I was still attempting to house train her. I had read that dogs can use word association very well and can even be taught to pee and poo on command – something I was very sceptical about until I met Laurel. Every time I thought she needed to "go" I placed her on the newspaper and when she began doing her business I would say "wee

29

wee, wee wee," or for a poo the words "something else". I would do this even if she missed the paper, praising her when she got it right and saying nothing when she got it wrong. It doesn't matter what words you use as long as you are consistent and sensible. However, if you think about it, if you decided to use the words "well done" for when you wanted your dog to poo, imagine the commotion that would cause if your pet were at a friends house, did something amusing and everybody shouted "well done". This could obviously cause problems so we must have a sensible choice of words for this task. I knew there would inevitably be mistakes but the key is perseverance and with Laurel I had all the patience in the world.

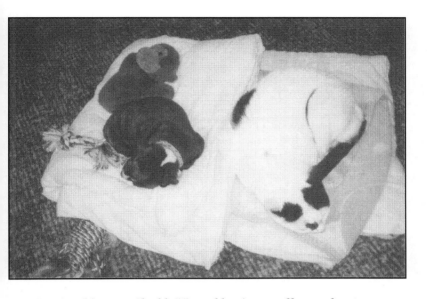

Harri and her new "buddy" Laurel having a well-earned rest.

CHAPTER FIVE

FIRST VISIT TO THE VETS

A few days later I was off to the vets with Laurel to have her checked over and discuss spaying and micro chipping. The micro-chipping of any pet, I feel is very important, not only so it makes it easy for animal and carer to be reunited should one or both of them get lost but also it may prevent certain people "dumping" their pets once growing tired of them. Micro-chipping, in my opinion should be law. The spaying I only knew about as I had taken Harri for the "snip" after watching her come into season the first time. I had to remain completely silent in the house as any movement or sound would send Harri into frenzy. It was quite hilarious watching her strutting around with her bum skywards making really weird, high-pitched noises. At the time when I lived in Old Catton, she was an indoor cat (due to the near by main road) so I didn't have to worry about any Tom cat chasing after her but the whole ritual surely couldn't be very pleasant for her. I was assured spaying would stop this and more importantly, could prevent certain cancers in later life so this was the course I took. I needed to discuss this with the vet to see if the same thing applied to dogs.

On our first visit to Catton Veterinary Clinic, I decided that as Laurel had had no inoculations I would keep her safe in Harri's cat transporter. I placed her inside with a warm blanket and her "cuddly". As I walked into the surgery the first sight I was greeted with was, what looked like a massive Staffordshire bull terrier. Of course looking back now it wasn't massive at all but it just looked that way compared to Laurel. I looked at the chap with the staffie and said, "I've got the same as you but just the smaller version" to which we all had a bit of a laugh. I looked at the other staffie and I remember thinking if Laurel grows up like that one she'll be a fine looking dog. She did and she is.

We both sat in the waiting room for a while, Laurel nearly asleep and me making a fuss of the other animals until Lenka the vet came out and called "Laurel Moore" which I must admit tickled me a little. When I took Laurel out of the basket and placed her on the table there was a huge "ahhh what a pretty little face" and as soon as Lenka picked her up for a closer look Laurel gave her the obligatory washing of the face with her tongue. She was wriggling with excitement trying to get to Lenka although she had one eye firmly focussed on me. Lenka gave Laurel the "once over" and said everything was absolutely fine even though the dog was mad (her words, not mine). We discussed the spaying issue and I decided that the pluses far out weighed the minuses especially when the evil "cancer" word was mentioned again. I never intended to let Laurel breed so I decided it was the best thing. This, I was told could be carried out at around nine months of age. Lenka also advised that I started training as soon as possible to get Laurel used to the words, if nothing else. As Lenka said, she may not take any notice of the words at her age but she would get used to hearing them. The bedroom sleeping arrangements were also a definite no no!. Just like little children, if she got used to it she would be very difficult to move so I had to have a re-think on that one.

Before leaving I made the appointment for her first injections. When we arrived home, as Laurel was now wide awake it was playtime so for half an hour we fought with each other until she finally decided to go to sleep. Peace!

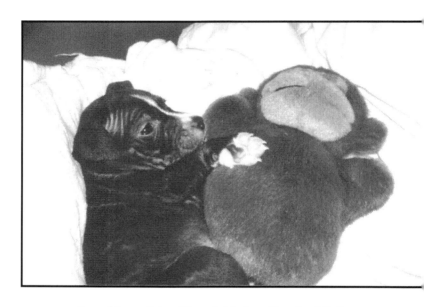

Laurel (complete with wrinkles) and her "cuddly"

CHAPTER SIX

TRAINING

Although Laurel is the first dog I have ever had I can honestly say she was and still is so easy to train. I'm not sure if it's because I do it the correct way or if she is just a very receptive dog but either way it's very easy. The first words I had to get her used to were "wee, wee" and " something else". Everytime she did her business I had to say either of those words so she would associate doing that with those words. I think house training has to be one of the top priorities and it didn't take Laurel long to master it.

I started by laying a sheet of newspaper down and if she did make a mistake (which will obviously happen) I would lift her onto the paper and say the words (to correspond with what she had done) If she got it right, however, I made a big fuss of her and gave her a "treat" (a small piece of biscuit) It didn't take her long to work out that if she went to the paper and do one long wee she would only get one treat but if she went several times she would get several treats. She would therefore run to the paper, do a little squirt then run back for her treat. She would carry out this manoeuvre probably five or six times, each time getting a small treat and even when she could do no more she would go to the paper, crouch down and still expect another treat. Even today (especially when it's wet or cold outside), I will say "come on let's go outside and do a wee, wee" and she will go outside, crouch down quickly, do

37

nothing then run back in for a treat. I have wised up to this little game now so I will watch her.

The other main word I wanted Laurel to know and obey immediately was "leave". Having read all about the Staffies reputation I thought this should be her most important training session. Any bull terrier, through instinct (dating back from days when they were bred to fight) is able to lock its jaws and almost nothing can prise them apart.

I remember reading a newspaper story (believe it if you will) of a Staffordshire bull terrier who sunk his teeth into the arm of a man and would not release. After several people tried to prise its jaws apart with wood and even a crowbar the only way they could open his jaws was by smashing the poor dogs head between a car door and the steel door frame. The car door was left badly damaged and I fear the poor dog died. This taught me a valuable lesson. I needed to know 100% that Laurel would release her grip on my command whatever she had between her teeth. Sadly if the owner of the Staffie in the story had taken time to teach his dog this it may still be alive today. I remember my son Steven and me having a good laugh with his dog, Arnie one day. Arnie had his toy in his mouth and I tried everything to make him let it go but with no joy. Steven said, "I know how to make him leave it" and with that produced one of Arnie's treats. Even then Arnie was in two minds whether to let go of the toy and have the treat but eventually the treat won the day and he let go of the toy. Something we both laughed at but it could have had much more serious consequences if it had not been a toy Arnie had in his jaws.

38

I began the "leave" training sessions almost immediately with Laurel. I started by picking her tugger (this is her toy consisting of lots of pieces of a strong string type material tightly woven together which I use to play tug with her) and playing a game with her. When she was sufficiently interested (tugging hard and playfully growling) I would say "leave" and prise her jaws apart. As she was still very young I could do this but even at that age you could feel the strength there. I did this several times a day until one day she did it all by herself. She had her tugger gripped very firmly and I was pulling her when I said, "leave" – her jaws opened immediately. I felt so proud and I knew this was one word we had to keep practising on and I still do so even today. It never ceases to amaze people that one minute Laurel will have her toy firmly in her grip, growling ferociously with me tugging at it but as soon as I say the word "leave" her jaws open immediately. The word doesn't have to be said firmly or aggressively, infact you can even whisper it with the same end result. This is also a command she will take from anyone. Once she has let go of the object she will sit down and raise her left paw. Luckily I have never had to use this command in anger but it's comforting to know that it's firmly etched in Laurel's mind.

The next thing to teach her was to sit and wait for food – this one was going to be fun! As Lenka the vet had pointed out, it was never to early to start the training sessions and although all of these things began to take shape over a number of weeks, I really do feel I benefited by starting early with Laurel. When Laurel's food was ready there was no holding her back (I think this was because she had been used to fighting off all her brothers and sisters to get food before she came to live with me). I would hold Laurel in one arm and place her food on the floor with the other – that was when the fun began. She would wriggle like a worm trying desperately to get to her food but I held her back saying "sit, paw, stay" and I don't think she heard a word. All I could hear was the scrapping of her feet on the floor and her desperately grunting trying to get to the food. This one was going to take a bit longer I felt. I was right! We went through this ritual every mealtime for weeks until one evening I placed her food down and she didn't actually put up much of a fight (I think she was getting used to the fact she didn't have to battle to get her food). It was then I could make myself heard so I said, "sit" and gently pushed her backside down. I did try the "paw and stay" but by this time her head was buried in amongst her food. I now felt I was getting somewhere though. I did begin to become a little concerned with her eating habits. She would literally scoff all the food down as quickly as possible until her tummy resembled a barrel almost ready to burst. In fact sometimes she could hardly walk. After quick phone call to Lenka, however, I was assured it was perfectly normal for young puppies to look this way after food. Laurel did gain a new nickname though – "Balloon Belly". It was so funny watching her waddle around after her meal. After a few more weeks of food training it was finally coming together. When I placed her food on the floor Laurel would sometimes sit without my command. If she didn't I gave the command and gently pushed her bottom to the floor. I would then say "paw" and lift up her left paw (this was just to make her do something before I rewarded her with food). When this had been completed she was allowed to dive into her food. Before too long she was doing all of this by herself with no prompting from me. I also wanted to make sure I was able to touch her food or even remove it

40

from her while she was eating it. I've heard many people say they would not dare go anywhere near their own dog if it had food. That may be very well if you are pre-warned but if a stranger had no idea or a small child approached the dog while it was eating, who knows what may happen. Small children find big cuddly animals fascinating and even more so when the animal is feeding so again being on the cautious side and knowing the Staffies capability I wanted to be assured this situation would not cause any problems. I began by gently placing my hands in her food bowl while she was eating – no problems at all. It was then I crouched to her bowl and pretended to eat from it – this time she just backed away. I dread to think what anyone would have thought if they had seen me carry out this training session. I still carry out these practises today and no matter how hungry Laurel is or if its her favourite food (chicken) she will always back off if anyone goes near her food. On this, as in many things I trust her implicitly. As the weeks went on the training became more rewarding with Laurel becoming better by the day. I tried to make all the training sessions interesting for her because once any animal loses interest you can kiss goodbye to the attention. The sessions were relatively short and sweet with plenty of rewards for correct behaviour and no punishment for wrong behaviour. As I stated earlier Laurel was an easy dog to train.

*"Balloon Belly" having an afternoon nap – The other
"Balloon Belly" in the photograph belongs to me.*

CHAPTER SEVEN

THE STORM.

As Lenka the vet had pointed it out to me, Laurel's sleeping arrangements needed a bit more thought. First of all I had thought of leaving Laurel's dog bed in the kitchen but on closer inspection there were far too many chewing temptations in that particular room. A lovely wooden dinning table and chairs, a welsh dresser etc, etc. What fun a mischievous little pup could have in that room! I thought it would be best to situate her somewhere where temptation was completely out of reach so by the time she had grown to adulthood (I'm still waiting for that after six and a half years) she would not feel the urge to chew and destroy things. I decided the best place to put her bed would be the porch area so I set to work making a minor conversion. Firstly I had to fit a radiator and also a child gate so she would know that when it was shut she must stay there. This was all part of my house and the only time she really spent there was night time and when I had to go out but I tried to make it her own little home. There was also absolutely nothing she could chew in that room – or so I thought. When I was at home she had the run of the house.

On the first night in her new "bedroom" there was lots of whimpering when I left her but as Lenka had said using the old cliché, "you have got to be cruel to be kind" so sadly I had to walk away. The whimpering soon subsided and I knew she was asleep which now meant I could do the same. I think she must have slept better than I did because

I didn't hear a sound all night. In the morning she was her normal bright and breezy self, running around the house like a madman, chasing Harri up the stairs and Harri chasing her down the stairs. The following evening, however, was a different tale. After putting Laurel into her dog bed she went to sleep quickly as did I, but during the night a storm blew waking me immediately. Laurel was crying, not whimpering but crying loudly. My first thoughts were to leave her to go back to sleep because if I went to see her now, she would expect it all of the time. That thought lasted all of about ten seconds. I couldn't bear to hear this little dog only a few weeks old crying so I went downstairs. As soon as I walked into her bed area she made a run for me so I immediately picked her up to reassure her. With that she almost got inside my tee shirt I'd slipped on. I tried for over half an hour to lay her down coaxing her back to sleep but the noise from the wind outside would not allow her to do so. I wasn't going to fall into the trap of taking her back to my bedroom so I sat on the floor, laid her on her quilt, picked the whole thing up and began rocking like a child. Within minutes Laurel was asleep. It was then I made Laurel a simple but solemn promise. I actually said to her " I promise you, that me and you are going to have so much fun together" something I feel is still being fulfilled today by both parties. The storm subsided and nothing else was heard from Laurel that night.

Laurel soon got used to the various noises she would hear during the night and only on very few occasions would she ever wake up barking or whimpering Even when I disturbed her either leaving for work or coming home early in the mornings she would just go outside, do her business,

44

come in and to go straight back to sleep. She knew that the area where her bed was, belonged to her and when the small child gate was closed behind her she knew she had to sleep or lay in her bed. Only on very rare occasions did she ever complain about being left there although on one such occasion she made it more than clear she didn't want to be there.

Upon arriving home from work one lunchtime – when Teresa was not around – I noticed something different about the porch window as I stopped outside my house but I just couldn't put my finger on what it was. As I unlocked the door I noticed Laurel laying on her back, tail wagging frantically and ears down. By this time I had gotten to know some of Laurel's mannerisms and I knew that this pose – especially with the ears down – signified one thing. She had done something wrong. On closer inspection of her area I noticed just what was wrong with the porch window – the curtains had gone! Obviously feeling very bored (not a good situation for a Staffie to be in) she decided not only to pull the curtains down but also to drag them into her bed and sleep on them. I had read that it's a pointless exercise scolding an animal long after the event, as their memory span is very short so in effect it will not know what it's being told off for. This is definitely not so in Laurel's case – she knew exactly what she had done and was probably thinking on the lines of "wait till your father gets home" All I had to say to her, quite calmly was, "whose done that!" and just as happens now she rolls on her back, ears down and wagging her tail. The only thing I don't like about these actions is that sometimes she shakes, even now when she's done something wrong, almost like she is shaking with fear. In fact, if a complete stranger saw her do this I can only assume they would think the poor dog has received several strong beatings. Anyone that knows me, however, will know nothing could be further from the truth. To my mind beatings do not work as punishment for animals. With these words Laurel knew she had done wrong so I felt no further punishment necessary. The curtains, however, were in dire need of repair. I didn't want to replace them because this could have been a new game Laurel had invented – luckily not so as there was no repercussion of the curtain incident. I really thought I covered all exits, so to speak, as for as chewing temptations in her bed area but I had neglected to think of the curtains. The only other things she found to chew in there was the side of her bed and the plastic radiator knob and with both occasions she had the same actions of laying on her back etc. when I walked in the door. I must admit both times on seeing Laurel do this my eyes went immediately to the curtains. I did find plenty of her small teeth in her bed so one can only assume, like babies cutting teeth, they tend to chew on things. In fact at one point I was finding teeth all over the house. I was beginning to wonder if she would have to have a set of dentures!

Something to chew on?

CHAPTER EIGHT

ANOTHER BIG DECISION

Laurel continued to progress day by day with very few problems. Harri and her were getting along nicely with plenty of playing but no aggression. Harri would occasionally fire a warning shot when Laurel got a bit too close for comfort but generally they loved each others company. Laurel's training was now showing very positive results and sleeping arrangements suited all.

The time soon came around for Laurel's first injections. Carrying her into the vets, she was greeted with the usual "what a pretty face" and oh how old is he?" – everybody naturally assumes every dog is a he. As soon as anyone started showing any sort of affection to Laurel she wriggled like a worm, trying to get to him or her and once that was achieved the wash with her tongue quickly followed. Nobody appeared to mind though. Once again Lenka examined Laurel saying everything was fine except "she was mad" and injections followed with no problems at all. We returned a few weeks later for the second dose and it was then the wait for something I had really been looking forward to – the first walk outside. I had been getting Laurel used to a lead and collar in my back garden with mixed results. Sometimes she wandered around with me as though the lead was not there but other times she fought to remove it. I think it depended on what frame of mind she was in.

As soon as enough time had elapsed to allow the inoculations to be effective Laurel and I were off out into the big wide world. There we were wondering along the path outside my home with me saying all the normal words of command that I knew she must learn. "heel" when she pulled, "sit and stay" at the road edge and of course "good girl" when she got it right. She wandered from one side of the pavement to the other not quite knowing what was going on. This was all very new to her – and me for that matter – and she seemed so excited by it all. Of course virtually every person we passed gave an "ahh – isn't he lovely" with Laurel loving all this newfound attention. If anyone dared to stop to make a fuss of her she jumped all over them with excitement – something she still does today – licking and wagging her tail. This is one trait I just have to put down as a Staffie trademark as most of the Staffie's I know are the same over excitable dogs. Not all but most of them. This is one piece of training I think must go down as a slight failure as I could never stop her going crazy with people – even complete strangers. I put it down to her being a very happy and excitable dog. Lenka, on the other hand puts it down to her being mad. We walked all over the estate with Laurel enjoying every second of her newfound freedom.

The lead training wasn't really working but it was to be expected on her first outing. Every time we came to the roads edge I would make her stop, sit and wait for my command before she proceeded to cross. At that point in her life she had not a care in the world. If any other dogs were around, Laurel certainly never took any notice. All she was concerned about was to gain their owners attention – which most of the time as a puppy she did. After our first walk together Laurel slept for about two hours – under the watchful eye of Harri.

As the weeks went by she became used to the collar and lead and her daily walks around the estate. One thing I did have to purchase however was a training harness as she was very prone to pulling on the lead even to the point where she would choke. I tried various ways of holding her back but she was becoming so strong so I thought it best to "nip it in the bud" before it got too out of hand. The training harness is an excellent piece of equipment that actually goes around the dog's chest so it makes them much easier to control. It certainly made a difference with Laurel. It made lighter work for me and also prevented Laurel from choking.

One Saturday afternoon Teresa and myself had an invitation to her parents for tea. I never had any time for Teresa's stepfather – I found him arrogant, moody and was of the opinion that everybody had to make the effort to talk to him while he made no effort at all. I initially made every effort but realising the chip on his shoulder was too big I gave up trying. This did become acutely embarrassing when Teresa and her mum were out of the room as myself and Terry sat in silence. This was certainly no hardship on my part, as I really didn't have anything in common with him anyway. Teresa's mum, Carol, was a lovely lady and a wonderful cook so the offer of tea was accepted straight away but we did have a small problem – Laurel. This would not normally have been a problem but only a few weeks earlier Carol had had to make the awful decision to have her own dog, William, put to sleep. William, with age not on his side, was suffering from heart problems that were worsening and was now starting to have severe fits

51

and Carol was told by the vet that William was suffering. He had now gotten so bad he could hardly walk. She telephoned me to talk about what she should do but I fear I was no help in this situation whatsoever – all I could do was listen. She telephoned the following night very tearful saying she had been to the vets that day so I immediately realised the sad choice she had made. Carol was absolutely riddled with guilt and sadness. I did my best to reassure her that what she had done was for the best and William would not have to suffer anymore. All Carol could think off was, would he have made a recovery had she not had him put to sleep but sadly and truthfully the answer was no. I listened to her talk about her faithful friend for some time and I have to admit unbeknown to Carol I had tears in my eyes on more than one occasion especially as I glanced down to Laurel and Harri asleep together on a blanket. I think the most moving thing she said was, when the moment came to take William to his final visit to the vets she produced his lead and the poor dog thought he was going for a walk so he staggered to his feet the best he could and even managed a slight wag of the tail. This, of course broke Carol's heart. She vowed after William she would never have another dog. Remember the statement "when you buy a dog you buy heartbreak".

The dilemma I had was should I take Laurel over to Carol's so early after she had lost William. The last thing I wanted to do was to upset Carol after her very traumatic and upsetting few weeks. On discussing this with Carol, however, she insisted I take Laurel so that small problem was averted.

We arrived at Teresa's parents early Saturday afternoon and upon entering the house I saw something I don't think I had ever seen – Terry almost laughing and the cause of this – Laurel. We walked in and I immediately let Laurel off her lead as she was almost choking herself through pulling with excitement. Of course she ran straight into the lounge where Carol and Terry had just sat down with a cup of tea and a slice of cake. The sight I was greeted with had me in hysterics although initially Terry didn't look very happy about it at all. Laurel had headed straight for Terry who had a cup of tea in one hand and cake in the other so he was powerless to fend off anything let alone a mad Staffordshire bull terrier! Laurel was straight up and running around his shoulders stopping for a split second to wash his face with her over active tongue. Her tail was wagging frantically and she was literally going round and round his shoulders with Terry frozen with both arms out stretched. Carol burst out laughing so this was the cue for Laurel to do the same to her. To see this spectacle you would assume Laurel had just found her long lost friends – the fact that this was the first time she had met Carol and Terry had absolutely nothing to do with it. We all had a good laugh and as soon as Laurel had slightly calmed (hardly at all really) Carol made a real fuss of her. Looking back it was probably perfect it happened that way as it didn't really give Carol an opportunity to get sad – she was laughing so much at Laurel. Also Laurel had achieved something I thought was impossible – she had made Terry laugh. The only time Carol grew a little sad was when Laurel began sniffing around the house obviously smelling where William had been.

Carol, Teresa and myself had a pleasant afternoon chatting and watching some TV. Terry was his normal moody self even though it was obvious Carol was upset about the previous weeks with William. Laurel had performed the impossible by making Terry laugh but not even she could perform a miracle and keep him happy all afternoon! After a lovely roast cooked by Carol I decided to take Laurel for a walk on a field that was only a few yards away from the house. This would be the first time laurel had been for a walk away from the estate where we lived. We left the house with Laurel again pulling as though she knew exactly where she was heading for. As we approached the field I decided we should walk around the perimeter. It was when we were about half way round I thought about letting her off her lead. I had heard so many stories of people doing this and their dog running away never to be seen again. My good friends, Graham and Margaret had told me their dog Holly would run and not come back for ages. The thought of letting Laurel free scared me especially as she was still very young. What if she ran and didn't come back? She was still young and in a strange area. What if she ran in the wrong direction and onto the main road? After all she still had no road sense. Pushing these thoughts to the very back of my mind I decided to give it a go. I was talking to her all the time as I bent down and unclipped her lead from her collar. Now she was completely free and could go anywhere she wanted. Talking to her all the time I walked ahead slowly. It was then she walked about five paces if front of me, stopped, turned around and waited for me to catch up. As soon as I was by her side she did exactly the same manoeuvre. Walked, stopped, turned around and waited. This was the pattern of our walk. I couldn't believe how good she was and on reflection she was probably as worried as I was when I let her free. Maybe she was thinking it was me that was going to run away. This little walk with Laurel free from the lead and the many more after it proved two things and these things are still true today. When I let her free there is no way she will run away from me and also even if I wanted and was able to, there is no way I could get away from her. I felt so proud of her that day I just had to go back to Teresa's parents and tell them all about our walk.

We left Carol's and Terry's later that evening and I was happy in the knowledge that not only had I discovered that I could trust Laurel off her lead now but that I felt I had also done some good in making Carol a little bit happier although that was down solely to Laurel. I think we can safely say everyone liked her – even Terry liked her.

Laurel settling down for the night.

CHAPTER NINE

LETTING GO?

In the May of that year when Laurel was about 16 weeks old the inevitable happened, Teresa and myself called it a day. It was something I always knew would happen, as we were so different in many ways. I was 36 at the time and she was 25 (eight years older than my son) but the big difference was, in many ways she was still a child. It's often been said that I have never grown up but there are occasions when everybody has to act sensibly and like an adult – boring I know but it has to be done. Teresa, unfortunately was incapable of doing this at any time and it wasn't long before we both realised we were heading in no particular direction so we had to call it a day. I was particularly upset as it meant I would probably not get to see her mother, Carol again and this was one person I did like very much. I went over to Carol's house for a chat and to say my goodbyes shortly after Teresa and I split. Carol had decided to get another dog – a Spaniel and she said it was mainly due to me taking Laurel over to hers that Saturday afternoon that had help make up her mind. This made me very happy and I could tell this was easing the pain of loosing William. Carol told me I could visit whenever I pleased but under the circumstances I thought it best not to. We said our goodbyes and I left.

Our split did leave me with a major problem, however. With Teresa not around anymore and me working 12 hour shifts, who was going to see to Laurel? Having chatted with

Geoffrey, the vet I was told that the night shifts would not be a problem (although not an ideal situation) as she would be asleep for most of the time but 12 hour day shifts were a different ball game. As she was still very young I could quite easily get her used to being left at night and Geoffrey assured me that she would be able to 'hold' herself for 12 hours. The only option I had for the day shift was to come home at lunchtime (something I didn't think the company would be to happy about) to let her out. I must admit I was very unhappy about both situations and I did hold my hands up and say, maybe I should have given this a bit more thought especially as Teresa and myself were never really going to be permanent. If I wanted to keep Laurel, this system had to work.

To be honest, Laurel got used to this very quickly and didn't appear to mind at all. I couldn't help but feel terribly guilty though as she had to be left for 4 twelve hour shifts per 8 day cycle. This certainly wasn't the way I had intended it to be. On rare occasions she would wet or mess on the floor but that was to be expected and as her porch area was tiled there was no harm done. I got the usual "mad" greeting when I came home – unless she had done something, in which case she would be on her back, ears down and wagging her tail. She was so good when I came home from work in the mornings after a night shift. Although she had been left for 12 hours and was so excited to see me, she would go outside, do her business, have a mad five minutes playing with her tugger and then go straight back to sleep allowing me to do the same.

On my four rest days from work Laurel and myself had a lot of catching up to do. This was our cue for some fun. We

58

spent hours playing, fighting, and going for walks. The training sessions continued and were working exceptionally well due to Laurel's quick learning ability.

Towards the end of May/beginning of June Teresa and I had a Holiday booked to the Greek island of Lefkas. Obviously, after our split, Teresa and myself would not be going but I now had a spare ticket. A very good workmate of mine, Clive decided to accept the invitation so it was all systems go for a real "lads" holiday. This would not be a problem as far as Laurel was concerned as I had already planned to put her in kennels for two weeks. I had thought all of this through before deciding on a dog and my way of thinking was, providing a very good kennel home could be found there should be no need to give up a once a year holiday. This was something else I wanted to get Laurel used to at an early age. I travelled around several kennels until I discovered Bomaris Kennels near Marham in Norfolk. Having had a good look around I was very pleased with the facilities and the lady owner who it was quite clear had a real, genuine love for animals. This had to be the one. Although this all seems very well thought out I knew I would desperately miss Laurel and I also knew she would desperately miss me so it was with mixed emotions I approached the holiday.

With the issue of leaving Laurel for two weeks and the fact that being on my own again meant leaving her when I went to work I started to convince myself I was not being fair to Laurel. Although she was now used to the fact that she had to be left I was not overly happy with the set up and thoughts were entering my mind I never thought would. Was it fair to keep her? As much as I idolised her I wasn't sure if I was doing the best for her or just being selfish. Would she be happier without me? With these thoughts in my mind I reluctantly took Laurel over to the kennels the day before my holiday to Lefkas. I would now have two weeks away to come to a decision I never thought I would have to make.

A very early picture of Laurel and me

I always made the promise to myself that the one and only reason I would ever consider letting Laurel go would be for her sake not my own.

Upon arriving at the kennels Laurel was as excited as ever. As soon as we were out of the car she was pulling in every direction on the lead waiting for the first person to come into view. It wasn't long before the lady that runs the kennels came to greet us and Laurel gave her the now famous Laurel greeting. Jumping, licking frantic tail wagging etc, etc. When the lady said, "we've got a live wire here haven't we" I thought to myself "you don't realise how live yet!" We went through the formalities of registration, vets numbers and contact numbers before I was asked to take Laurel to her pen. This, at that time was one of the hardest things I'd had to do as it felt to me like I was leaving her behind forever. I was feeling especially bad as the thoughts of letting her go were still buzzing around my head. As we walked past the other dogs in their pens Laurel hid behind my legs for protection. I lead her into her own pen and crouched down to make a fuss of her. It was at that point I think she knew there was something wrong because she jumped at me licking my face and almost getting into my lap. I put her in the little dog bed, told her to stay and walked out of the pen. As soon as I shut the netting door she was out and forcing herself against the door trying to get to me. This broke my heart. I walked out looking and talking to Laurel as I did so and I still maintain to this day it's one of the most difficult things I have ever had to do. The kennel lady was very good and realising I was a little upset she reassured me that Laurel would be well looked after and she was sure the kennel girls would absolutely adore her – of that I had no doubt. After a little discussion on Laurel's good and bad habits and the food she preferred I left missing Laurel as soon as I got back into my car.

Harri was no problem at all at that time, as she would go to my parents while I was on holiday. That evening going back to my house with no Harri and no Laurel was a very lonely evening and Laurel was on my mind all night. It was the first time we had been separated since she came to stay four months earlier.

Clive and myself fly out to Lefkas the following day with me worried about Laurel but still determined to have the perfect "lads" holiday. After being there a couple of days I had made my decision. Every time myself and Clive had a meal, be it just a snack or the full Monty, I found myself looking at the floor towards my feet – just where Laurel would be laying if I was at home with her. There was no way on this earth I could ever give her up and I couldn't wait to get home to see her. I knew I would have to deal with the situation of her being left but that was just what I would do – deal with it and not take the easy option. I telephoned the kennels several times while I was away and was assured Laurel was fine. In fact the kennel lady said "she's doing everything that I want her to do" I thought to myself "that's my Laurel" I also telephoned my mum to tell her the decision I had come to – one which I think she was just as pleased with as I was. With that decision made I enjoyed the rest of the holiday. It turned out to be one of the best I have had – a laugh from start to finish with Clive – still a good friend and one of the most genuine people I know. I do feel, however, if I had not made my decision early on in the holiday maybe I wouldn't have enjoyed it as much as I did.

Two weeks later I arrived home late in the evening so it was too late to fetch Laurel but I was to make that my first job in the morning and I couldn't wait to see her. I was at the kennels at 9 o'clock sharp the following day and was greeted by the kennel lady. We quickly sorted out the financial side and I asked just how had Laurel been. She said at first she could tell Laurel desperately missed me and seemed a little depressed but after a few days with the young girls who worked there she seemed to perk up and soon became "everyone's favourite". Other than that she had been absolutely no problem at all. I heard one of the young girls coming down the corridor I had taken Laurel down two weeks previously and the way she was talking I knew it was Laurel she was fetching. All I heard her say was "come on my little favourite, hang on, don't pull, wait a minute, he's not going to leave you this time". With that the door burst open – by the sound of it from a butt from Laurel's head – and she caught sight of me. That was it; she was all over me, licking play biting, and generally causing absolute mayhem. It was so good to have her back and by her actions she felt the same way. Everyone present had a good laugh and all made some sort of comment about missing Laurel and about going to have a lie down in a darkened room. Laurel and me were reunited once again and it felt right.

Laurel Asleep Under Harri's Watchful Eye

CHAPTER TEN

LAUREL'S FIELD

It was shortly after I arrived home from holiday and Laurel and I were reunited that, on one day during our normal walk around the estate we came across several large fields all interlinked with each other. I always knew the fields existed but I was totally unaware that you were able to walk dogs on them until this particular day when I saw several dogs on the fields. As these fields were literally 10 minutes walk away we decided to investigate further. We discovered there were probably six or seven fields all together, some with various crops, others with nothing but it was obvious they were used by dog walkers even if only around the perimeters of some of the fields. The fields lead directly onto land which belonged to Norwich City Rugby Football Club so I knew if we ventured that far – which we frequently did – I would need a good supply of poo bags, just in case. No farmer or field owner has any problems with dog walkers so long as their mess is cleared up so this is something I have always taken very seriously. Once again a few spoil it for the rest, though.

This very large field area soon became known affectionately as "Laurel's Field". We spent many happy hours on the fields meeting all kinds of dogs and all kinds of people. Sadly on passing the fields recently I realised it now contains several houses. The rugby club still remains but Laurel's Field is now one big, ugly concrete jungle. Although we have now moved from that area of Norwich it

65

still brought a lump to my throat reminiscing about all the happy hours we had spent together on Laurel's Field.

Be it rain, wind or shine, if Laurel and I were not to be found at home the surest bet was Laurel's field. When we left for a walk Laurel knew exactly which direction she wanted to head and she would frantically pull on her lead until she reached her destination. Sometimes I would try to fool her by going to her field but in a different direction but it wasn't long before she got to know that all roads lead to her field. It was on one such occasion that whilst walking around the fields we came across a partly fallen tree. The reason that this part had fallen was because the growth had begun to die off for some reason. This obviously meant that the wood was quite brittle so I decided to break a small piece off and throw for Laurel. She was like a child with a new toy and every time we were on the fields after that day she would run directly to the old fallen tree and wait for me to break her new stick off. She would then run a few yards in front, stop and then begin to destroy the branch with her teeth. She would take small chunks from the wood and just spit them on the floor. This would continue until virtually nothing was left. I soon stopped this practice after one day I saw her running with a stick protruding end – on out of her mouth. Thoughts of the end of the stick hitting the ground while Laurel was still running made me think again. Also, I didn't relish the thought of having to pull out splinters from her throat after she had chewed a stick to pieces. For days after this, however, Laurel still stopped in the same place and waited. When I carried on walking saying "no" she would soon follow with other things soon occupying her mind.

By this time I was a lot more confident about Laurel being free from the lead. I could never do this on the estate, as, like today, Laurel has absolutely no road sense. I tried from the very beginning to instil in her the danger of the roads but unfortunately when Laurel is out of the house she has tunnel vision and can only see her destination and not the hazards in front of her before she gets there. For that reason the only time she is free from the lead when we are out is on fields or parks. When on the field she would run several yards in front of me but always turning round with just a glance to see if I was still there. Sometimes I would let her go and stand still myself and when she turned and saw I was either a long way from her or that I was not moving she would run back to me as fast as she could sounding like a herd of elephants. I would also let her go and then hide behind a tree waiting for her to notice I was not there. Every time she would run back to find me. I once even tried walking backwards to try to confuse her but as soon as she realised I was getting further away rather than closer she ran towards me.

There was one occasion, however when Laurel did run away from me and would not come back even when I called her. It was just another sunny day on Laurel's field when we were both taking in the sunshine, the peacefulness and the countryside. Without warning a very large Alsatian came 'through' one of the hedges that surrounded the fields and stood a few yards in front staring at Laurel. Now, Laurel is very good at acting brave and very good at chasing things that run away from her but I had a feeling this dog was going no where. Laurel would chase cats in the garden and as most of them obviously ran away she would continue chasing very bravely. If, however

67

a cat were to stand its ground she would always stop before she reached it. If the cat moved in her direction she would be the one to turn tail and run. The same thing happened with the birds in the garden. She would always weigh up the opposition and if she felt it would retreat, she would give chase. If she didn't win the psychological battle she would come to me for back – up. After about a ten second stand off with the Alsatian, Laurel realised the psychological battle was lost and made her way, gingerly in between my feet. She sat down with the thought, no doubt, of "if you're taking me on, you're taking us both on" I must admit the Alsatian didn't look aggressive, more playful and inquisitive but Laurel still sat with me not knowing what to do. The Alsatian then made a run toward us and before I could pick Laurel up she was gone with the other dog close on her tail. I screamed for her to come back but she just carried on in the opposite direction with the Alsatian in close pursuit, luckily not in the direction of the road. At this time I didn't know what to do. Within seconds a man appeared (obviously connected with the Alsatian) dressed just like you would imagine an old Norfolk farmer to be. On seeing the panic in my eyes he said, in a broad Norfolk accent, "Don't worry boy he's only playing – he wouldn't 'urt a fly". "That's all very well but my f*****g dog is probably about three miles away by now!" was my reply. With that he whistled and within a minute his dog was by his side but where the hell was Laurel? Obviously I need not have worried because no sooner had these thoughts entered my mind I heard a rustle in the tall grass. I could see the grass moving and I knew it could only be one thing. She made her way back to me but in a very large circular motion so she would have to go nowhere near the Alsatian. She was soon sitting back in between my feet.

68

After having a quick chat with the 'farmer type' man and apologising for my language we were on or way – no harm done. I was quite pleased this had happened in one way as it signified to Laurel that she was not always 'the guvnor'. It did make me smile when the man and his dog walked away Laurel stood and walked two or three paces toward them as if to say "I sorted that one out" I wonder what would have happened had the dog turned around at that point? I think we all know the answer to that one.

On another such occasion whilst walking on Laurel's field she had a little scuffle with an English bull terrier and this time I think she was the 'guvnor' albeit the English was about twelve weeks old at the time.

Over the weeks while walking on the field we met several different people and several different dogs. One such person was a young girl with an adorable English bull terrier. I can't recall the girl's name so I will call her Jane but the dogs name was Daisy. Daisy would always come to me for a fuss if Laurel was out of the way but would soon retreat when Laurel returned. Many times I would stand chatting with Jane about ten feet apart, with Laurel sitting between my feet and Daisy between Jane's feet. Neither dog seemed bothered about the other but just did not want to mix. As I once pointed out to Jane, these dogs that are supposedly 'fighting' dogs can sit ten feet apart with no problems at all so that must prove these particular two did not want to fight. We did this on numerous occasions and there was never a problem – not until Daisy's brother Billy arrived on the scene.

One day while walking on the estate with Laurel we came across Jane and Daisy and their new addition. Inside Jane's coat was a seven-week-old English bull terrier puppy she had called Billy. I just had to stop to see him so with the usual performance of Laurel beside me and Daisy beside Jane I held the little pup. He was absolutely adorable and Jane said she couldn't wait to take him to the field when he was a bit bigger. To be honest neither could I.

About a month later Laurel and me were as usual, walking around the field when in the distance I noticed Jane and Daisy. Also in tow I saw another dog running around who I assumed was Billy. As we got closer I realised my assumption was correct because running around all over the place was Billy. Now about three times the size (and now larger than Laurel) since our last meeting but still very much a puppy. Very large 'ploddy' paws and into everything that moved and most things that didn't. As we neared each other Laurel took up her usual position in between my feet and Daisy did the same while Billy was wondering around aimlessly looking to cause havoc but being very weary of Laurel. After chatting with Jane for a few minutes about Billy he suddenly realised I was there and made a move – the wrong move – and came over to me to investigate.

The proud Queen of the field

"This field belongs to me – but I don't mind sharing it"

Realising he'd only came across to have a nose I called his name which made him even more excited. As he got to within about three feet of me he took off to jump up at me purely in a playful manner but unfortunately he never reached as far as me. On seeing Billy jump, Laurel took off as well and in mid-air, caught Billy with a head-butt any street fighter would have been proud of. There was no growl, no aggression, as such but just a clash of heads. As Billy flew backwards he gave a small yelp – more from shock than injury – and fell on his back. Laurel stood over him with her shoulder muscles bigger than I had ever seen them and a look on her face that said " go on son try that again – make my day" I apologised to Jane but could not tell Laurel off as all she was doing was to protect me from what she saw as an attack. Billy was totally unharmed although a little shaken and Jane was fine with the situation. Daisy remained where she was and didn't move an inch. I now realised not only did I have a good friend in Laurel but also a protector. That day Laurel was the 'guvnor'.

We often came across the trio on the field and it always followed the same format. Laurel beside me, Daisy beside Jane while we talked (mainly about the dogs) and Billy wandering around. After the little skirmish however, Billy kept well clear of Laurel - and of me.

After another venture to the field shortly after that incident something happened that had me worried the Police would pay me a visit and this time it was nothing Laurel had done.

While heading for home, Laurel and me were approached by about four or five young children around six or seven years old. Laurel has always loved children of any age and she appears to be gentler the younger the children are so upon seeing the children her tail started to wag frantically. Staffies are sometimes nicknamed the 'nanny' dog because of their love for children and this is true of all the Staffies I have come across. With more than one child approaching Laurel, I think she must have thought it was her birthday. When the children saw her one of them, quite sensibly asked if he could touch her. "Will he bite me mister?" he said. "You've got more chance of me biting you than her", I replied. There was an absolute look of horror on all of the children's faces. I quickly had to reassure them I was only joking and that " no, there was no way she would bite anyone and more importantly, nor would I." With that they were all making a fuss of Laurel, who by this time was over on her back enjoying every second of it. We left with all the children waving goodbye to Laurel and completely ignoring me. As we carried on walking I began to think. What if the little boy went home and told his parent's I'd threatened to bite him. With these days of political correctness exploding out of control, anything could happen. I had visions of being carted away by the Police for threatening to assault a child. I could see the headlines "BULL TERRIER OWNER THREATENS TO BITE CHILD". Nothing ever came of the incident and although a bit of a worry for me, I'm sure it was taken the way it was meant. We bumped into the same children many times and they always stopped to make a fuss of her and always called her by her name. A funny incident that, in these days of political correctness could have turned nasty.

It was also around this time that several other of the smaller children around our area were beginning to notice Laurel and on realising the sort of reaction they would receive if they coaxed her, would always make an effort to come and see her. My next-door neighbour's daughter, Nagine and her two friends Charlotte and Jacob often knocked on my door to ask, "Can we see Laurel". Nine times out of ten I would fetch Laurel to the door where she would absolutely adore all the attention. She would literally climb all over the children trying to lick them and the children would be in fits of laughter. When they had their little bit of fun they would all wave goodbye and say, " See you tomorrow Laurel". This carried on nearly everyday until I moved from that area of Norwich and on the day of the move, Nagine's mother told me that Nagine had been crying the night before because she was going to miss her friend Laurel. I had a feeling Laurel would miss them too.

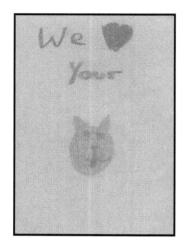
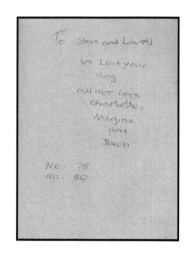

This handmade card was put through my letter box shortly before we moved house.

The wording says *"To Steve and Laurel. We love your dog. All our love Charlotte, Nagine and Jacob. No. 78 and No. 80.*

CHAPTER ELEVEN

OPERATION TIME

When Laurel reached around ten months old, on advice from two vets, Geoffrey and Lenka at Catton Veterinary Clinic, I decided to have Laurel spayed. I had thought long and hard about this and after discussions with the vets I decided that the positives for having this done far out weighed the negatives. I never intended Laurel to be a breeding dog and when I was told that, as nearly everything concerned with reproduction (the womb, the ovaries, etc.) is removed on spaying it did alleviate certain cancer risks in later life.

When we arrived at the vets early in the morning, Laurel was her normal over excitable self hardly being able to wait to get through the vets doors. By that time, Sue, the receptionist was getting used to the sound of Laurel's feet on the wooden floor and although she could not see her from behind her desk she would look at me, smiling and say," Laurel?" and then ask us to take a seat. After watching the other animals at the vets, be it dog, cat, rabbit or budgie, I realised one thing – they all looked petrified. Even when taking Harri to the vets she would begin meowing loudly as soon as we entered the reception area. Laurel was certainly an exception to the rule – she loved it because so many different people surrounded her. On this particular occasion I had an early appointment with Geoffrey and then Laurel was to be left for the rest of the day for her operation. While waiting to be called Lenka came through from her surgery room to reception and on seeing Laurel said " I see Geoffrey's got the short straw today". She walked across to make a fuss of Laurel with her responding immediately by rolling over on to her back. Lenka was talking to her all the time saying things like "you're not supposed to be happy in this place – we're used to seeing frightened dogs not happy ones" This caused some amusement to the other clients waiting with their animals shaking beside them.

After going through the formalities with Geoffrey and signing consent forms I handed Laurel over to a young girl who worked there. I crouched down and gave Laurel a kiss and she was taken through to the back of the surgery. I didn't realise until that time how difficult it was going to be leaving her again and I did have a shed a tear or two when I arrived home. I was also surprised at how quiet the house was without her even though she had only been living with me for ten months.

That day became one of the longest ever. I was continually looking at the clock. I'd been instructed to ring at about 2pm and all manner of things went through my mind until then. Laurel was just like my child. I now realised how my parents must have felt when I was a young child having to leave me in hospital waiting for the operations I had to have. I began reliving those times.

I had one operation when I was about two. This was for a small rupture in my stomach and obviously I don't remember much about that one. I then had to have an operation on one of my eyes at the age of four. There are certain elements of that one I remember quite vividly. I remember going hysterical when my parents visited. I remember crying at night and I remember my mum always looking like she had been crying when they left me. The last operation I had I remember like it was yesterday and whenever I tell the story I get quite emotional. If it had not been for my mother I would not be here writing this book – that is an absolute fact.

When I was about seven years old I had to have an eye operation to correct a 'turn' or squint in my eye. To simplify this, the procedure was to shorten the chord attached to my eye and my eye muscle. I was scared from the first day I knew I had to have this done. On the day I was due to go into hospital mum and dad did the usual thing of being very brave and reassuring but I new they were both deeply upset and very worried. I don't think we give children the credit they deserve when it comes to observation – they notice everything no matter how quiet you are while talking or how good an act you're putting on – children know.

I was taken to the Norfolk and Norwich Hospital by my parents at around lunchtime and after checking in I was told mum and dad could take me to the dinning room for some lunch. At that time, 35 years ago, there were no children's wards as such and the only division was between male and female. All of the male rooms and wards were one side and the females on the other so the male dinning room was full of men of all ages. At the time, me being only seven years old they all looked terribly old and although they all went out of their way to make me comfortable I was so scared. At that point I was the only child in a room full of old men so they decided to put me at the head of the table. I remember being offered some soup, which I ate as quickly as I could, even burning my mouth, so I could get away. My parents left and I didn't find out until many years later that my father turned and looked at me at the head of the table and almost came back to get me. After this, mum made sure I had my food in my room as, not wanting to return to the dinning room with the old men I was refusing food. Looking back now, maybe the men weren't that old but just seemed that way to me – a young child and they were all very pleasant to me offering fruit whenever I saw them. To me though it was a very frightening experience.

I was dreading the operation and I remember the day I was due to go into theatre mum came to visit. I also remember waving to her out of the window as she left and shouting "think of me this afternoon mum". This must have broken my mum's heart but she didn't let it show. I was taken down to theatre and the nurse told me that there was a little girl having the same operation next door to where we were and she was sitting on the nurse's lap. When I asked if I could do the same she told me I was far to big and brave for that – if only she knew. I remember the small injection in my left arm and the doctor asking me to count to ten. I got to four and that's all I remember about the operating theatre – on that occasion. I awoke in the middle of the night just so happy that the operation was over. The following day my parents came to see me and found me so happy because the operation was all over. As soon as mum looked into my eyes and told me to follow her finger going from left to right and back again the expression on her face changed and I immediately new something was wrong. Mum tried her best not to give the game away but left the room returning with the surgeon, Dr Norton, who had performed the operation. He carried out the same tests mum had done and said "fine". I can hear him saying that word now "fine". Mum, however still didn't look happy though and disappeared from the room again. About twenty or so minutes later she returned with a nurse I had been seeing on a regular basis at the N&N Hospital. After a very brief set of tests the nurse left without saying a word, closely followed by mum. When mum returned a few minutes later I knew for definite something was wrong, as she had been crying. She tried desperately to hide it but I knew. It wasn't until my parents had left that the nurses and doctors started running around that I realised it was serious. I was asked how much I had eaten that day and told not to eat anything else. I remember a nurse sitting on my bed and a young boy called Paul who shared my room standing in front of me eating from a Ritz biscuit box. The nurse told him not to eat in front of me and when I enquired why I was told I had to have another small operation. To say I was devastated is an understatement. I was distraught. I was still very drowsy from the previous operation and the next thing I remember was waking up crying as I was being wheeled into theatre. Once again the injection was put into my arm with me still crying and I made no attempt this time to count. When the injection took effect though it gave me a really strange feeling. My tears that were around my eyes and running down my cheeks suddenly became hot, my eyes dried up and I was out like a light.

What transpired was after the first operation the previous day the stitches attaching the chord to my eye muscle and my eye had broken. The operation had been performed to shorten the chord but unfortunately the stitches didn't hold and we were told later that my eye muscle had slipped back into my head 2 inches so my eye was, in effect attached to nothing. Obviously this was potentially fatal. My mother noticed this immediately and had it not been for her persistence I honestly believe I would not be here today. The surgeon could see no problem and it was only when the nurse came in after being pursued by my mother, that they realised something was seriously wrong and they had to rectify it as soon as possible. Of course this mishap meant I had to stay in hospital longer than expected and as this ran over the Easter period mum and dad brought my Easter eggs to the hospital on Easter Sunday and laid them all out on the empty bed next to mine. Chocolate was and still is, always guaranteed to make me happy.

I often asked my mother why she didn't tell me I had to have another operation and she says I was so happy that she just couldn't do it. She didn't want to upset me again. She did her very best trying to hide her tears but I knew. I just knew.

At exactly 2pm on the day I took Laurel in I called to see how she was and if everything went well with her operation. I was told everything was fine and she was resting but I could pick her up at about 5.30 that evening. At that time in my life I didn't really believe in God but that day I did thank him for keeping her safe. I was at the vets to collect Laurel at around 5.15pm. When I called to the reception I paid the bill and was told Laurel would be with me shortly. It was then I heard the scratching of the floor – it had to be Laurel. The door opened and there she stood held on a lead by a young nurse. She had what appeared to be, an over sized surgical collar and looked very drowsy from her operation. On seeing me, however, her eyes widened and she made a move for me but with the effects of the anaesthetic still in her system she fell over. This was such a pitiful sight I was reduced to tears. The nurse said to me "don't worry, you're not the first and you won't be the last to shed tears in here". I took Laurel straight to the car and we went home.

As soon as we arrived home Laurel went to sleep while I had a read of the numerous leaflets I had been given on "do's and don'ts" and "things to look out for". The main thing was to ensure exercise and climbing of any sort was restricted until the wounds had a good chance to heal. With the massive operation she had just undergone I didn't think she would be able to exercise because of the pain she would be in. I was later to be proved wrong on that one though. After a few hours asleep she woke so I made her a little food. Under the leaflets instructions, a little chicken and rice – chicken just happens to be Laurel's favourite – but she ate none. She was walking into everything with this massive surgical collar on so I decided to remove it. It would be no problem if I were there to watch her. She then wandered into the kitchen to where her food was so I naturally assumed food was the thing she was after. Suddenly there was, what sounded like a herd of elephants running up the stairs and the same herd of elephants running down again. Laurel had decided to chase Harri up the stairs and Harri had decided to chase Laurel back down again. I just couldn't believe what I was seeing. Only hours after a major operation and she was running up the stairs. I quickly ushered her into the lounge and into her bed, where she slept again. We both slept in the lounge that night. I needed to be sure she was alright.

I soon overcame the problem of Laurel not eating the following day. In the morning Laurel was very stiff and obviously in a bit of pain and again would not touch the chicken I prepared for her. She would soon dive into Harri's food bowl and eat Harri's food though. So without Laurel seeing I lifted Harri's bowl and filled it with the chicken I had prepared for Laurel and placed it back down in Harri's food place. When I turned away I saw her out of the corner of my eye looking at the food and looking at me. She was gradually getting closer to the food and then with a lightning dash she dived into the food bowl and finished it off thinking she'd got one over on me. She walked away, ears down, licking lips (all the tell tale signs that she had done something wrong) and headed towards me. I couldn't do anything but laugh. The end result had been achieved even if it meant a little deceit from yours truly.

Laurel made an excellent recovery and within a few weeks the stitches were removed and she was back to her normal manic self.

It wasn't too long after this I met another girl named Debbie. This was to cause more problems than anyone could ever imagine.

CHAPTER TWELVE

JEALOUSY

I met a girl called Debbie while out one evening and it wasn't too long before she was introduced to Laurel. Of course, Laurel loved her – she loved everybody. Every time they met Laurel would go crazy and Debbie would appear to enjoy the commotion she caused. However, shortly after she met Laurel a couple or so times I noticed a change in both her and Laurel when they were in my company. Laurel tried more and more to get between us when we were sitting together and Debbie seemed more and more to be pushing Laurel away. Not in a deliberate act but subtly moving her away from me. It wasn't too long before I realised I had a problem that need sorting before it got completely out of hand. I realised Laurel was vying for my attention because after all for the last nine months she had got used to it being just me and her and now there was a new kid on the block. With Debbie, however it was just plain jealousy, which I think she would have had, even if my pet had been a rabbit or a hamster. She grew to think I was put on this earth specifically for her and nothing else so obviously there was, at some point, going to be a clash. Given that Laurel was, to me, my child and to be fair we had been through quite a bit in our relatively short time together, I thought Laurel's reaction was quite natural. All she could see was a stranger taking me away. Debbie's behaviour however confused me. Was it not possible for me to care for more than one person or thing in my life? After all I was and still am very close to my parents and at that time my Nan who was still around then. As the weeks went on the problem appeared to worsen with Laurel getting in between us more and Debbie pushing her away more and inevitably arguments between Debbie and myself started. I must stress that on no occasion did I see Debbie be nasty towards Laurel. If I had witnessed that be sure that I would have said something to her. I tried my best to talk to Debbie about this but at that time it fell on deaf ears as all she could see was me showing a little 'mutt' more attention than her. With hindsight I think she was probably right but I do think a less insecure person like the wonderful woman I am with today would have maybe been able to accept it for what it was. My love for Laurel didn't mean I thought less of anyone else.

Shortly after I met Debbie on November the 27th 1997 a tragedy occurred that put all of this into relative insignificance – my dear old Nan passed away suddenly and the help I received from Laurel was something I will never forget.

CHAPTER FOURTEEN

MY DEAR OL' NAN

I have deliberately missed out chapter thirteen in this book as; if my Nan were around today (her being the most superstitious person I ever knew) she would never forgive me for writing about her in Chapter 13!

I was always very close to my Nan and Granddad – or 'Nesty' as I used to call him. This came from my school days when a few friends and me used to talk backwards so we could have a private conversation wherever we were. My granddad's name was Ernest so I turned that into 'Nestern' and this soon became shortened to 'Nesty' – a name he is still referred to by family members today. I never knew my grandparents on my mother's side as my grandmother, May, passed away many years before I was born and my Grandfather Sidney, passed away when I was about two. I do vaguely remember going to visit him when he was in an old peoples home shortly before he passed away. Nesty passed away on February 12th (also his birthday) 1992 and this hit me very hard. He was diagnosed with cancer shortly after Christmas and was taken into the West Norwich Hospital in the beginning of February but basically by that time it was far too late to do anything and he passed away on what would have been his 79th birthday. The day before both Nan and myself had sat by his bedside all day and a good part of the evening while he slept restlessly. My poor Nan was obviously distraught when he left us. They had been married almost sixty years and had never spent a night apart until he was taken into hospital. At his funeral I sat beside my Nan in the car behind the hearse and when we stopped outside the crematorium she was helped out of the car by various people and my father and her other son, my uncle Eric went to walk by her side to enter the church. My Nan stopped immediately and said "No - I want Stephen by my side" This, of course was absolutely no disrespect to my father nor my uncle but it was just a sign of how close she was to me. In the crematorium we cried together. When I left her later that day I told her I was going to get 'hammered' she smiled and said "That's exactly what he would have wanted – have one for him" I did.

On Sunday November 27th 1997 I was at work on my first day shift. I was in our workshop when my office phone rang. I knew it was an outside call and not and internal one as it had a different ring tone so I went to answer it. My mum was on the end of the line and by the tone of her voice I immediately knew something was wrong. She said "Steve, I don't know how to say this but I've got some very bad news – it's your Nanny, she's died" I remember slipping back into my chair, punching my desk and shouting "no!" She had been staying at my uncle's house and had gone to bed as normal the previous night but when he went to take her a cup of tea in the morning she had gone. I had to leave work after this tragic news – there was no point I being there in that sort of state so I informed whoever needed to be informed and went to see mum and dad. After a cup of tea and a few tears I decided I knew exactly where I wanted to be – at home with Laurel.

When I arrived home about 11.30 Laurel knew immediately there was something wrong. She came to me licking my face almost as though trying to cheer me up in her own way. I cried again and this time Laurel licked my tears away. After an extremely large Brandy I filled up a small hip flask with the same and we walked to Laurel's field. We wandered around all of the fields with Laurel in front always checking to make sure I was there. On this particular day even she didn't appear to be in her normal playful mood. She plodded around aimlessly almost as though she was aware of how upset I was. With the Brandy now starting to take effect all that was on my mind was my Nan. I could just see her sitting up there (that place called heaven which I never used to believe in) being re-united with Nesty after five years of desperately missing each other. I could hear Nesty moaning and Nan returning the compliment. They always moaned at each other but we all knew how much they loved each other and now they were back together again.

The hip flask of Brandy didn't last long but it was something I needed at the time. It's works for some and not for others. I am just one of those people that it appears to help. Note I did say ' appears' to help. When we reached the main part of one of the fields I noticed a crowd of people so I gathered there must be a Sunday League football match. This meant I had to put Laurel on her lead rather quickly because if she caught sight of the football I knew exactly what she would do. With a small tennis ball she will put the ball in her mouth and bring it back so if it didn't belong to her I could tell her to 'leave' and then give the ball back to it's rightful owner. A large ball like a football, however, was a different story. Although she couldn't get this in her mouth it wouldn't stop her trying so she would go wherever the ball went. I have seen her go straight through hedges, gardens and almost into a river trying to get her teeth into a football. Of course, if it's a soft plastic football she could puncture it straight away. On this particular day I clipped her lead on and we both went to watch the football match. Laurel made no attempt to get to the ball whatsoever. She sat patiently beside me watching the game almost as if she were taking care of me. I didn't feel confident enough to release her from her lead though – I had visions of her running away with the ball being chased by 22 footballers and me. We left the field as the match finished and headed for home. The two-hour walk with just Laurel and me had done me good although I was now slightly the worse for wear from the Brandy. When we arrived home I carried on drinking to numb the pain and think of the nice memories I had of Nan.

One of Nan's frequent phrases after my many bouts of tormenting her was " You'll miss me when I'm gone" to which I would answer, "no I'll just find someone else to torment". We would have a good laugh and the tormenting would continue. I think now my dad has taken over as prime target as far as the tormenting stakes are concerned. It was exactly the same with Nesty. I remember on so many occasions we would sit and watch the football results on a Saturday afternoon and let's say Norwich beat Ipswich 2-0 (I can't think of a better example) the result would be announced Norwich 2 Ipswich 0 followed by the rest of the results. About half an hour later I would say something like "that was a bad result for Norwich then" to which he would reply "what do you mean they won 2 – 0. No they didn't they lost 2 – 0" would be my retort. " Look, we've

90

just watched it on the tele and they definitely WON 2 – 0"
"NO they LOST 2 – 0". This would go on and on and as
someone once pointed out to me I just chipped away like a
little Jack Russell nipping at somebodies ankles. Then I
would notice he'd be deep in thought and I would think
"gotcha". He'd then say "well who scored for Ipswich
then" to which I would erupt with laughter. "You little
sod" would be the nicest response I would get. I got him
every time without fail. Even though he'd sat through the
results I had him believing he'd got them wrong. All totally
harmless fun.

The one real tinge of guilt I had concerning my Nan was
about a week previous to her leaving us I was driving
home when I thought I'd call in to see her. Then almost as
quickly as the thought came, I began thinking that I was
too busy and I would visit her the following week – that
week never arrived. I do, however, have very fond
memories of the last time I saw her. My son, Steven was
here and Nan was in an old peoples home for two weeks
while my uncle Eric and his wife Eva were having a
holiday. On this particular day I intended to take Steven
back to his home in Wickford so I decided we would visit
Nan so he could say goodbye. When we arrived at the
home we went to Nan's room where she sat doing her
cross-stitch. She was so happy to see us both. After we'd
had a chat and Steven had said his goodbye's Nan asked if
I would push her in her wheelchair into the day room so
she could have a yarn with the other old folk. Bad move
Nan asking me to push you. We took the bends like Damen
Hill with Nan swaying from side to side shouting, "slow
down, slow down" so I did an emergency stop. Everyone in
the room including Nan had a good laugh and one of the

elderly women said to Nan "Is this your Grandson you've been telling us all about", to which she proudly said "yes and this is my great Grandson". She seemed so proud. After a kiss goodbye Steven and I left and as we reached the door we glanced back to see Nan smiling and waving. That's the last picture I have of my dear ol' Nan.

I was promised Nesty's wedding ring when anything happened to my Nan and it's been on the little finger of my left hand since that day. Nan wore this ring after Nesty passed away and although it has very little financial value it's probably one of the most precious things I possess.

Although it has been said that my Nan could be a 'funny old bugger', which I have to agree with, I think the good in her far out-weighed the not so good and I still miss them both dearly today. I look forward to seeing them both again – one fine day.

For the rest of the day after Nan left us, I have to confess I drank quite heavily until I finally crashed out on my sofa. When I woke in the morning with the sun shinning through my lounge window I looked to my side and there was Laurel. She had been lying by my side on the sofa all night.

CHAPTER FIFTEEN

EARLHAM PARK

The following months came and went in a fairly uneventful manner with me still seeing Debbie but hoping things between her and Laurel would get better. As I have said, she was never cruel to her but I just had the distinct impression she didn't like her and I'm equally sure Laurel felt the same way (unusual for Laurel as she liked everybody). By now though, it was definitely a case of love me; love my dog because Laurel was going nowhere – not without me anyway.

The following June Debbie and I decided to take a holiday to Zakynthos in Greece – something I wasn't really looking forward to because it meant leaving Laurel at the kennels again. I thought this time it wouldn't be so heart wrenching as we'd done it all before. In fact this time turned out to be worse than the last. I decided I would take Laurel to the Bomaris Kennels where she had been before because I really couldn't fault the place or the staff. On the morning of taking Laurel in she knew immediately something was going on and would not leave my side from the moment I got up. Whichever room I was in, Laurel was behind me – even the bathroom. Debbie decided she wanted to come to the kennels with us, something I was not too happy about as I wanted to spend a bit of time with Laurel on my own before I left her. When we got closer to the kennels Laurel became more and more agitated sensing what was about to happen. Trying to take her mind off things I pulled over to a lay-by and took Laurel for a quick walk in some nearby woodland. This annoyed Debbie for some reason, almost as if she wanted to dump her off as soon as she could. After our walk we arrived at Laurel's holiday home with lots of fuss for her from the excited staff. We went through the same procedure as before and after I had taken Laurel to her pen I returned to the office for a chat with the kennel lady. After sorting out the formalities I quickly darted back for one last goodbye for Laurel. This, I fear, was a big mistake. As I walked down the corridor past the other dogs, some of whom were barking and some contently sleeping I heard Laurel crying. I was heartbroken. When I reached her pen she pushed so hard up against the netting I thought she was going to come through. I put my fingers through to reassure her but to no avail. Ever since being a puppy Laurel's left eye has, on occasions been slightly watery but on this particular day it looked exactly like she was crying real tears. I quickly said goodbye and left, now with tears of my own. As I walked back to the office I caught the end of a conversation between Debbie and the kennel lady. " He doesn't like leaving her does he?" said Debbie coldly. " He just loves her" was the kennel lady's response. I remember thinking at the time, that statement summed it up – ' I just loved her'. I didn't expect any comfort from Debbie and I didn't receive any. After all Laurel was just another mutt to her. When I left Laurel I was absolutely certain of one thing – there was no way I would ever leave Laurel again at the kennels. This was no reflection at all on the actual kennels because they were fantastic and so were all the staff. I knew, however, Laurel was not the type of dog that would settle in a place like that. She was the type of dog that needed lots of attention and it was not possible for the staff

94

to concentrate on just one dog, no matter how much they liked her. If it meant no more holidays abroad for me, then so be it.

The holiday to Zakynthos came and went with me telephoning the kennels several times to make sure Laurel was ok – much to Debbie's annoyance. When I arrived to collect Laurel she, again went absolutely crazy with excitement that I'd come home. There had been absolutely no problems apart from her 'wetting' a little during the night. This was put down to the stress of being left but I began to wonder if it went a little deeper than that. Laurel never left my side for weeks after I arrived home.

It was around this time that I noticed my parents appearing to become more and more attached to Laurel. They had always made a huge fuss of her but they now seemed attached to her, which I thought was wonderful. They had even offered to take Laurel for the two days of the week I had to work. This was fantastic news as it now meant she wouldn't be left on her own for my 12hour day shifts. The two nights were no problem as she slept most of that time anyway. Laurel loved going to my parents as they live near a really large park and they looked after her like their grandchild. Her two days at my parents consisted of long walks in Earlham Park, playing ball in the back garden and laying in front of the fire. She enjoyed every second of it, as did my parents. My mum has often said that Laurel has done herself and my Dad more good than anything else ever could have. She got them out exercising, walking many miles and she also kept them occupied. An occupied mind is a healthy mind. Of course I would miss Laurel for these two days a week but I knew it was best for her this way and also good for Mum and Dad. They all had lots of fun on Earlham Park with Laurel running for miles, chasing squirrels and birds. Again, chasing things that run away from her seemed the most sensible thing to do. If it stood it's ground it was no fun for Laurel. As soon as the word 'squirrel' was mentioned, even in quite conversation, Laurel would be off like a flash searching around the trees to find one. I often wondered what would happen if she ever caught one, something one day we would all find out. On this particular occasion, on a day off for me, I decided to go for a walk onto Earlham Park myself with Laurel and my parents.

Earlham Park is a lovely place where I grew up. My friends and myself spent many happy hours as children in Earlham Park. Looking for conkers in the autumn, football in the summer evenings and basically getting up to all the tricks young children do. It's funny looking back, we were always being told off by the park keeper. I remember thinking at the time we had done nothing wrong but we were still being lectured. Then I thought we were children so we must be wrong and not one of us would dare to question what the park keeper had to say. When I look back now, however, nine times out of ten it was all harmless fun hurting nobody and I think the park keeper was just a grumpy old bugger picking on us children. We were never whiter than white but then no child is, but we certainly weren't as bad as the park keeper suggested. We did respect what he had to say because that was the way we were taught even though silently we all thought he was a grumpy old bugger!

On the day my parents and me decided to go to the park with Laurel it was a nice bright day and we walked virtually the perimeter of the park. About halfway I saw something small dart across the grass, completely out in the open. I quickly signalled to my parents to walk in the opposite direction in the hope that Laurel wouldn't see it. Out in the open with no trees around the baby squirrel had nowhere to hide. I was, however, too late, Laurel caught sight of the baby squirrel and belted towards it with me on her tail. I knew it was no good calling as all she could see and hear was the squirrel. Just as she had done on Laurel's field when the Alsatian chased her away she just kept going. The poor squirrel tried to run but it had nowhere to run to so eventually gave up and sat there rigid ready to take it's chances with Laurel. When it stopped running, however, Laurel stopped and looked at me for guidance. There was this baby squirrel a few inches long and a very much larger "killing machine" standing over it not knowing what to do - I do use the words "killing machine" in a patronising manner to all those who believe Staffies are that way inclined. When I reached them both you could see the squirrel was petrified so I used the words 'leave' and 'stay' on Laurel while I tried to remove it to safety. By this time my parents had arrived on the scene and upon seeing more danger the squirrel darted for my Dad. It ran straight up the outside of his trouser leg, up his coat, over his shoulder and was gone across the field in a flash. One of the funniest sights I have ever witnessed. So my thoughts on just what would Laurel do if she ever caught up with a squirrel were answered that day – absolutely nothing!

Tragically, Laurel's days on Earlham park are now over for reasons I will come to later.

On another such occasion while Laurel was staying at my parents we all thought she had some serious illness. When I telephoned my Mum to make sure everything was ok she said she was very concerned with Laurel's behaviour. She had been lifeless, refusing to go for her walk, sleeping most of the day and most worrying, not taking any food. When I arrived to collect her that evening after my second 12-hour shift I saw a different Laurel to the one I was used to. Normally when I walked in she would go hysterical. Her tail would wag frantically and she would be all over me. On this evening, however, I walked in to find Laurel on a cover on the sofa. As soon as she saw me she made a real effort to get up. She jumped to the floor gave a very weak wag of her tail then jumped straight back on her cover. It was as though she was saying ' I did my best'. I knew there was something wrong. When we got home I tried to get her to eat something but she was having none of it – not even her favourite chicken. As she was no better after a couple of hours I decided to telephone the vets. As it was out of hours I had to leave my number and a few minutes later I had a call from Geoffrey the vet. After explaining all the symptoms he said it was difficult to say what the problem was but it could be something as simple as stomach pains caused by something she had eaten in the garden and suggested that I left her till morning and see if she was any better. Also I had given Laurel her worming tablet the previous day so this may be upsetting her. I was assured that if she got any worse, Geoffrey would call to see her. Another night on the sofa for me ensued. I checked her several times during the night and she seemed quite content so I left her. In the morning she seemed slightly perkier and actually had a few pieces of chicken which was really positive. I gave Geoffrey an update and he said his assumption that she had eaten something she shouldn't have or the worm tablet was affecting her was more than likely the cause so no need to worry but keep an eye on her. After a few days she was back to her normal self.

At my parent's house Laurel discovered that the house whose garden adjoined the bottom of my parent's garden housed two lovely cats, Diana and Dodi - no prizes for guessing who they were named after. One morning while Laurel was wondering in the back garden she noticed a cat – Diana – on the three-foot high wooden fence at the bottom of the garden. The very 'macho' Laurel made a bolt for it but the cat didn't move, even when Laurel head butted the fence. It looked at Laurel in a "make me" manner in which only cat's can and deliberately slowly moved off the fence into it's own garden. A few days later Diana was actually in the garden sunning herself. Laurel charged towards her but Diana didn't move so when Laurel reached her they were nose to nose with the "I was here first" look from Diana. From that day they became the best of friends and could often be seen lying in the sun together. Dodi was a different matter though. He made one big mistake – he ran away. An almost identical situation arose with him. When her was in the garden Laurel chased him and he turned tail and ran so she naturally chased him. He cleared the fence without actually touching it closely followed by Laurel's head butt into the wood. I had a feeling he wouldn't venture into the garden again while Laurel was around and to my knowledge he didn't. Laurel got to know their names – if you said, "where's Diana" her ears would prick up and she would head outside. If you said, "where's Dodi" she would do the same but her back would be up. If Dodi had been slightly braver I think they could have been friends too. As the cats were quite similar in colour and markings it was quite funny when Laurel confused them with each other. She would bolt toward a cat at the top of the garden thinking it was Dodi but as she got closer realising it wasn't and more importantly it wasn't moving she would slow down to a walk and they would greet each other. It really was a lovely sight to see. I say 'was' because recently Diana and Dodi have moved home. Laurel still looks for her friend even now.

Laurel and myself outside Earlham Hall in Earlham Park

CHAPTER SIXTEEN

MOVING HOUSE AND HOME

In May of 1999, Debbie and myself decided to buy a house jointly but looking back now I realise it was for all the wrong reasons. I don't regret it because had it not happened I would not be where I am today and I would not be with the wonderful partner I am with neither. I don't regret anything that I have done in my life because I do believe everything has happened for a reason. I sold my house in Old Catton to virtually the first person that came round to see it although Debbie did have a little problem selling hers. We went ahead with the purchase of Layton Close in Drayton, Norwich even though Debbie's house had not sold. This was possible as at the time I was earning enough money to take on the mortgage on my own. This was my "get out of jail free card". Had this not have happened, when Debbie and I split shortly after it could and I'm sure would, have turned very ugly when trying to 'split' the house. As it was though she had no hold on it. Like I said, everything happens for a reason.

The house in Layton Close was not your typical house – it was more like a chalet – type bungalow. The interior needed lots of work as it all had very 60's feel to it. The extended upstairs was very small and to be fair the three bedrooms up there should have been one decent sized bedroom. The kitchen was very dark and needed artificial lighting all the time and the lounge, although quite large always seemed very cold. It didn't really feel like home.

The thing that really sold me the house was the garden. It was very large and had so much character. A large oak tree stood at the bottom with an even larger horse chestnut tree in the corner. Laurel bushes went all the way down one side and a row of conifers lined the pathway and a small section toward the rear of the garden. You could actually walk behind these conifers so it gave the impression you were entering another domain. The garden was well stocked with various plants but was in desperate need of some TLC. I could see it's potential and I wasn't proved wrong.

We moved in on May 9th 1999 with the first few weeks quite exciting. Laurel loved the garden, running round the conifers but not quite being able to work out how I was at the other side every time. I checked the garden perimeter for escape routes but found none so Laurel was completely safe in the garden – not that she would ever try to escape. Shortly after moving I decided to take Laurel for a walk around the estate so we could both familiarise ourselves with it and also to see if there were any other hidden places we could go for walks. We discovered a mobile home park that was surrounded with woodland, which seemed quite a popular place for dog walkers. Although this had no comparison with Laurel's field it would be nice to use as a change to the back garden.

I decided to leave the house interior and concentrate on the garden as the summer months were nearly upon us and one of the first things I did was to create an area that Laurel could use as a toilet area. I shingled a patch of ground towards the rear of the garden which I called my ' rubbish area' as this were the compost would go and the area I could have my fires. Laurel soon got use to using this area and seldom did she ever do anything on the lawn. When I opened the back door she would trot down the path beside the conifer hedging, sneak under the horse chestnut tree and do her business on the prepared shingle. Of course she was not too keen in the cold or wet weather but she soon got the idea of going underneath the tree to keep dry. On one such occasion Laurel (always leaving it till the last minute) bolted toward her toilet area, did her business and because it was cold, decided to run back indoors as fast as she could. Little did she know that lurking underneath the conifer hedging was Harri. As Laurel passed I saw this paw come out of the darkness, not a claw in sight, and take a swing at the passing Laurel. The 'body swerve' Laurel did was perfection itself although she did nearly hit the garage wall. I was in fits of laughter. Laurel returned to see where the paw had come from sniffing the hedging but by this time Harri was long gone. This happened on several occasions after that with Harri always being in the same position and Laurel always getting caught out. The funny thing was though, was after a while Laurel would run down the path and swerve at exactly the correct place even if Harri wasn't there and sometimes she would even check the hedge out on the way out so as not to be caught on the way back.

It was only a month after we moved in that something happened that made me realise that my relationship with Debbie and me living together was doomed before it started. After an argument over something that I cannot even remember she started screaming and shouting at me, which caused a great deal of distress to Laurel. Laurel started barking and jumping around – no aggression but clearly very upset at the situation. Debbie completely ignored her and stormed out of the house slamming doors on her way. Laurel, by this time was in a bit of a state and I was left fuming at what had happened. I am the first person to admit it takes two to argue but with Debbie it was so easy and she made it almost impossible not to. I was angrier at what she had done to Laurel and I firmly believe she had now got to the point where she knew by hurting Laurel she could hurt me. I would call that nothing short of evil. After not even a month Debbie had gone to stay with a friend for the night – something I was pleased about as it took a good part of the night to calm Laurel down.

When I look back at it all now, there must have been good times shared by Debbie and me but I honestly cannot remember them so it must say enough about our stormy relationship. The arguments continued and the upset caused to Laurel appeared to be worsening to the point where I knew something had to be done. I now began to notice certain changes in Laurel's behaviour. One thing she started to do was chase her own tail and initially I found this extremely funny. I remember an advert on the television where a terrier is shown chasing it's tail had the same effect – I was in hysterics at the sight of a dog pursuing something it couldn't catch. This was to turn into a serious behavioural problem that Laurel still has not rid herself of today – not totally anyway. Laurel was fine with me alone but as soon as Debbie appeared the tail chasing would start. Over the following weeks it worsened to the point of me considering the vet for help.

One Saturday evening Debbie (a.k.a Cruella De Vil) was up for a big argument with atmosphere in the house thick enough to slice in two. She had just arrived back from a

104

stay at her sister Rita's in Basingstoke, Hampshire. It was always a sure bet that after one of these visit's we would be in full argument within minutes of her arriving home and this time she didn't disappoint. Rita and her husband Tony were lovely people but I always thought that Rita belittled Tony by the way she spoke to him. He was almost like a lap – dog with "yes Rita, no Rita, three bags full Rita" and sometimes even I found it highly embarrassing for him. Debbie often tried this approach with me and failed miserably with an argument created out of thin air. On this particular evening Debbie was at her best and I shut Laurel in the kitchen because I knew Debbie couldn't care less about the mental damage she was doing to her. Debbie threw her usual tantrums, screaming and slamming doors, getting into her car, reversing out of the drive saying she was leaving for good, only to return ten minutes later for more of the same. I kept going into the kitchen to reassure Laurel who was, by now in a terrible state. I tried desperately to calm things down but appeared only to make things worse. Debbie stormed upstairs – peace at last I thought. I went to check on Laurel but she wasn't there. I checked the downstairs bathroom – nothing, the downstairs bedroom – nothing. I searched the house from top to bottom, even the little hiding places Harri had used in the boxes we used for moving – nothing. I then noticed the front door slightly open and my heart sank. Surely Laurel wouldn't leave the house without me by her side. Not in normal circumstances anyway, but these were far from normal circumstances. I walked outside into the darkness and called her name but saw nothing. With all the commotion going on she must have seen the front door open and ran away. I had to find her – she had absolutely no road sense and if she were heading for the main

Norwich to Drayton road she would not stand a chance. I ran along the close shouting her name knowing it would be difficult to see her dark tan colour in the dark. I was just praying she would hear my voice and follow it so I could take her home - nothing. I reached the bottom of the close and turned left – nothing. I reached the bottom of the road calling her name all the time – nothing. I was then on a 'T' junction and had no idea which way to go. It was then I thought I saw something move next to a wall about ¼ of a mile away. I shouted her name and saw the object move towards me – it was Laurel. I ran towards her calling her to come to me and by this time she was running in my direction. When we met I picked her up and squeezed her so tightly she let out a little yelp. I was overcome by emotion, sat on the pavement floor up against a garden wall with Laurel in my arms sobbing like a child. Laurel was licking my face frantically and I then thought how desperate she must have been to leave her home and me the way she did. This was the closest I had ever come to losing her and I now knew as far as Debbie and me were concerned it was over. This was the final nail in the coffin. When I returned to the house I let Debbie know in no uncertain terms my feelings for her although most of it was said in anger. At this stage Debbie and me both knew living together was not going to work so she set out to look for other accommodation, which she soon found with her ex-husband and her daughter. We carried on seeing each other occasionally but we knew the relationship was dead. As it was me that took the mortgage on I gave Debbie a financial settlement and we parted. The last I heard she had moved to Basingstoke to live with her sister. I would never go so far as to say all the trouble was caused solely by Debbie but I am an honest enough person to know that, on reflection most of it was caused by Debbie's own insecurities and far more happened between us than I am prepared to write about. Suffice to say that the relationship should never have happened and certainly not gone on the way it did. As far as Laurel was concerned, however, serious damage had already been done.

Mum, Diana and Dad, Roy with Laurel at my home in Old Catton

CHAPTER SEVENTEEN

DAVE

When a little cat turned up on my doorstep appearing very hungry I felt the need to feed the poor little mite. He was obviously very young – probably no more than fifteen weeks old – but was obviously very hungry. He was so friendly that I thought, although he had no collar on, he must be some body's beloved pet and they were probably out searching for him at that moment. I brought him indoors and fed him some of Harri's food, which he wolfed down like it was the first meal he had had for days. He guzzled the milk I laid down for him and then began exploring the house as though he was the new tenant. At this stage I kept both Laurel and Harri away from him just as a precautionary measure. I gave him lots of fuss while thinking about what I was going to do with him. My first thought was of that of the owners – I knew exactly how I would be feeling if it were any of my two missing. I thought the best thing to do would be to release him at the front of my house to see if he made his own way home. There was no problem with traffic as my house was at the very end of the close. Reluctantly I set him down outside but it was pretty obvious he didn't want to go anywhere. I closed the door and watched him through the window. He sat on the doorstep for half an hour 'meowing' loudly and pushing himself up against the front door. Then, without warning he made for the back garden gate scaling it with ease. I then began to wonder if he lived in one of the houses that backed onto my garden. I knew he didn't

109

belong to my neighbour John as he had far too much pride in his garden to own a cat. He often had a little 'dig' at other cats in the area that were constantly fouling up his vegetable plot. In fairness to him, he and his wife, Laura, they did have a wonderful garden and I would have been just as displeased as he was had it been my garden they were digging up. John and Laura spent most of their retirement time in their garden and it was a credit to them both. I didn't think he would belong to my other neighbours – Ray and Christine - either. Don't ask me why but they just didn't seem like 'cat' people to me. I decided to watch this little cat to see just where he was heading for. As soon as he saw my green 'wheelie bin' next to the garage, he was on it like a flash. He somehow managed to open it with such ease that it made me think he had done this sort of thing before – to the standard of becoming an expert at it. There he was foraging through the bin, obviously for more food. It was at this point I decided I would bring him in for the night and try more thoroughly to find his proper home in the morning. I found one of Harri's old blankets and made him a small bed in the utility room with Harri. She was a bit put out by this and appeared to spend most of the night on top of a cupboard. The little cat however seemed totally unconcerned by the ordeal and was soon asleep. Laurel soon went to investigate and as per usual was not that bothered, as the little cat didn't run away. I think it helped matters that he actually looked a lot like Harri – your typical moggy.

In the morning the little cat was hovering around the utility room bright and early, waiting for his food. He ate what I put in front of him with the same enthusiasm he had the night before. Now it was down to finding his 'mum and dad'. I thought it best to keep him with me, as it was obvious he didn't know his way home – if he had a home that is. I decided to make the relevant telephone calls to locate the missing owners – after all the cat wasn't lost the owners were. I telephoned all the places I would have been phoning had it been Laurel or Harri missing. The R.S.P.C.A., the Police, two of our local radio stations, Radio Norfolk and Radio Broadland and a couple of our local pet sanctuaries. I also placed a small card in my local shop window. Having left all the details and my name and number all I could do now was wait. The days went by with not a call from anyone about the little cat. The more I thought about it, the more it was looking like he was a stray that had possibly been abandoned. The way he scavenged for his food as though he didn't know if, when or where the next meal was coming from. The way he could expertly open a 'wheelie bin' lid in two seconds flat and the way he seemed in no hurry to leave, suggesting he had no home to go to. Also if somebody were missing a little cat they would have come across one of my efforts to track them down. The only thing that appeared to throw this whole assumption out of the window was how friendly he was to all and sundry. I could literally pick him up, lay him on his back and hold him like a baby – something if I tried with Harri I fear I would be nursing claw wounds for some time. These weren't the actions of a stray.

As time wore it was looking increasingly like the little cat had no need to find his home because he was already there. I tried again with the phone calls but all said no enquiries had been made. By this time him and Harri were the best of buddies and he was causing no problem to Laurel, although on one occasion while in the garden I did hear a

111

growl from Laurel's direction when the little cat walked past. It was almost an "I'll get you later when he's not looking" but they soon became friends too. I couldn't let the little mite go now so I decided to let him stay. Now for the name. It had to be Dave. Many people have said "why Dave" to which I always reply "he just looks like a Dave" That name stuck and Dave became a new member of the family.

Two things concerned me – what if an owner suddenly turned up? And what if Dave decided to go walkabout again and leave for good? I was pretty certain by that time that if he had an owner they would have shown up by now. On the second concern, that was something I would have to just live with and sadly it was Dave's built in curiosity that finally ended his short but eventful life.

Dave was an extremely inquisitive cat and after all his injections and having him tagged he was free to roam in the big wide world. It was a funny site to see first thing in the summer mornings when I went into the back garden and rattled a fork in a cat food tin. Immediately you would hear two cat collar bells coming from different directions unable to tell who was who. Harri, as now, would very rarely leave the garden although I knew Dave ventured further a field. As friendly as the two were they very rarely went together. They appeared to have their own pleasures and itinerary and would go their separate ways. It always seemed that wherever Dave was, he would manage to get back first for food, even though Harri was usually the closer of the two and I often wondered how many bins he'd been through on his nights adventures. He often came from the direction of John and Laura's garden, scaling the fence as if it wasn't there and although it was Harri that was often blamed for the poo flavoured potatoes, I know who my money would be on. It was quite funny to watch Laurel's face when, not one but two cats were descending upon her, that, from a distance she couldn't tell apart. It was a real double take and so funny to watch.

On May Sunday May 14th 2000 I got up as usual for work. Mum and Dad were to collect Laurel later that day for her two-day stop over so after making a quick fuss of her I went straight to the garden with the can and fork. As soon as I rattled it I heard the bell and saw Harri emerging form the back of the garden but I only heard one bell. I remember saying to Harri something like, "makes a change for you to be here before hungry guts". At that time I wasn't unduly worried, as Dave had on occasions been on a longer than usual jaunt it took him a few minutes to get home. As I fed Harri and waited for Dave I grew a little concerned as only on very rare occasions had he not turned up before I went to work. The time was now about five thirty and I had to leave for work so I laid Dave's food down and left. This is something I certainly couldn't have done had Harri been the missing one because Dave would have scoffed the lot. Harri, however only ate what she wanted and left the rest so I knew there would be some for Dave when he decided to come home after his night on the tiles. It was a lovely sunny day and I drove out of the close, to the bottom of the road and onto the main Norwich to Drayton road. I had travelled about a quarter of a mile along the main road and I noticed on the pavement on the opposite side of the road something I thought was a small animal curled up asleep on the kerb. I remember thinking to myself it was a strange place for an animal to sleep being

113

so close to the road. As I got closer I noticed it was a cat. It was then my heart sank. I was unable to stop immediately as there were cars behind me but I pulled over as soon as I could, turned the car round and went back. It was Dave. He lay on the kerb as though he was a sleep. He was curled up as I had seen him many times before but this time there was something wrong. He was stone cold. There was no mark at all on his body apart from a tiny piece of blood on his nose. He was dead.

To this day I will never know if this was one of his regular journeys or if he had somehow got lost but one thing I did know – he was along way from home, even for him. When I got Dave home I telephoned work to tell them I wouldn't be in and with many tears, wrapped Dave in a woollen blanket. I sat in my back garden holding him while Laurel and Harri wondered around the garden. Before I finally let Dave go I placed him on the floor so Laurel and Harri could see him. They both came to him and walked away. Heart-broken I buried Dave at the bottom of the garden where he had spent many happy hours. For days after, Harri was looking for her buddy spending hours sitting on his grave. It was also a long time before I got used to hearing only one bell in the mornings. When I moved from Drayton a few years later, I felt I was leaving him behind and his little grave was the last place I visited before leaving the house for good. I brought his small plaque I made for him with me and I still have his photo standing in my kitchen today. Most of all I still have the memories. Dave was such a character.

Somebody once commented to me that Dave must have thought all his Christmases came at once when he landed on my doorstep. All I can say to that is I hope I made his short little life as happy as he made mine because he certainly brought a lot of fun and laughter with him.

The one and only Dave.
This is the only photograph of Dave that I possess and like him, is deeply treasured.

CHAPTER EIGHTEEN

BEHAVIOURAL PROBLEMS

Although I was now living on my own again Laurel's behaviour was causing a great deal of concern. Her tail chasing and barking was getting to the point where, I have to confess, I thought it was out of control. When she was on her own with me she was very little problem but as soon as a third party was introduced she went crazy, chasing her tail and barking. It even got to the stage where she would persist with this behaviour if I spoke to somebody on the telephone. This continued at my parents when she stayed there for the two days while I was working but at that stage her behaviour there was not too bad – only when I arrived there. At that stage I had no option but to take her to see Geoffrey the vet.

Geoffrey's first concern was that there may have been a physical problem with Laurel's rear end, making her try to bite it but upon closer examination this was ruled out. Geoffrey also informed me that staffies were quite prone to this sort of behaviour but Laurel's case did seem extreme. It had to be a behavioural problem. It got me thinking that all of the trouble Debbie and me had had over the previous months had taken it's toll on the poor dog and I had to take some of the responsibility for that. I also had the responsibility of making her better. I made an appointment to see a dog behaviourist via Geoffrey to see where that would take us.

By the time I got to see the behaviourist, Emma Magnus, Laurel was worse than ever. She tended to sit by my side and whimper quite a lot and as soon as anyone else became involved in the conversation she was off, tail chasing and barking frantically. What follows is some of the basic report I received from Emma after our meeting.

REPORTED PROBLEM.

Laurel has been chasing her tail since she was a puppy but this behaviour has become a regular pattern over the last few months. The most likely time for it to occur is during the excitement of someone arriving at the house. There seems a link between the behaviour and the presence of Steve as Steve's parents rarely witness this when they are on their own with Laurel. (As I stated before, at this time her behaviour at my parents was not too bad.)

DIAGNOSIS AND MOTIVATION

Laurel is highly attached to Steve and it is probable that the behaviour manifests itself at times when she has had to share his attention or feels the need to gain it. Certainly in the past, this behaviour received a response from people – either because they thought it was amusing or that they were concerned there was something wrong with her. Either way Laurel has learned this behaviour is a rewarding behaviour that helps her deal with frustration but is also rewarded by the response of her owner.

TREATMENT ADVISED.

I have taught Steve the importance of ignoring inappropriate as positive or negative responses are often rewarding to a dog, as with children. I have suggested Steve should try to use punishment as little as possible, ignore more and praise Laurel for correct behaviour. I have advised Steve on how to reduce Laurel's over dependency upon his presence. This includes not responding to her attention seeking behaviour. Accustoming Laurel to periods of time separated from him when he is at home – keeping off laps and out of bedrooms. It is important to give Laurel attention when she is calm.

This is the basic gist of the report to which I agreed with most of but not all. There were also things I could do with Laurel's food to make her 'work' for it but basically I had to ignore her when she was seeking attention. Easier said than done. I failed at the first hurdle as far as Emma was concerned. While still discussing things with Emma Laurel began tail chasing and I was immediately instructed by Emma to ignore her, which I did. When Emma turned her back though I glanced down at Laurel and, thinking Emma was not looking, gave Laurel a discreet wink. Emma turned quickly saying, "Did you just wink at that dog?" " She's my buddy" was my only defence. After a tongue in cheek ticking off from Emma, Laurel and me left for home with a list of do's and don'ts that everyone had to adhere to if Laurel was to get better.

Although this new regime was extremely difficult to adhere to we all did our best, none more so than my dear parents. They carried out all instructions to the letter knowing this was all for Laurel's benefit. Whereas sometimes I would let little things go, Mum and Dad stuck to the rules rigidly – all credit to them.

Since I first brought Laurel home I have kept a brief record of her illnesses and visits to the vets. Not so much a diary but a reference book to check up on the frequency of illnesses she may have had or the remedy for such illnesses. A perfect example of this is every year around May time she tends to have lots of itchy spots that always require treatment from the vet. It's something to do with the time of year but now I have it on record I know when it's coming and what to do about it. I kept a record of her behavioural problems and what follows reflects exactly what myself and my parents had to endure, the sadness it caused and the outcome. What follows are excerpts from the reference book;

4.5.00
Appointment with Emma Magnus. Attention seeking. Given a list of do's and don'ts. She's definitely getting worse. Please help.
5.5.00
Trying all the methods Emma suggested. Still tail chasing. Very difficult and upsetting.
6.5.00
Mum and Dad collected Laurel a.m. She had been sick. Very good day – only chased tail twice. Carrying on with Emma's methods. Fingers crossed!!
7.5.00
Laurel only tail chase twice at Mum's but when I went to collect her she went into it big time. When we arrived home she was barking and tail chasing for almost an hour.
9.5.03
Barking and tail chasing when I stopped to speak to my neighbour. Pretty bad again when I am with another person.
10.5.03

Very good day. A friend of mine came to the house and brought her small baby. Laurel was very excitable at first but calmed down reasonably quickly. She was absolutely wonderful with Sally's little girl Alicia. All she did was roll over in front of her. Fingers crossed.

11.5.03

Only tail chasing occasionally. Great progress.

15.5.03

Laurel went to Mums. Behaviour is fine.

18.5.03

Appears to have had a slight relapse. Tail chasing and whimpering. Not as bad as before but still there.

20.5.03

Backwards a bit. Will not settle.

It was around this time that for some inexplicable reason Debbie turned up on my doorstep and true to form it wasn't long before she was looking for a fight. I tried my best to keep Laurel out of the way from this and asked Debbie to leave which she duly did.

5.6.03

Seems very lifeless and withdrawn. Was not happy at the reappearance of D. Neither was I!!

12.6.03

Off her food.

25.6.03

Very bad day. Constant tail chasing at Mum's for three hours. So bad that they had to bring her home and leave her on her own to calm down. When I arrived home from work there was no evidence that she had been doing this while

alone. (This incident really upset my parents as they began to think Laurel would never be able to stay with them again)
26.6.03
At home with me on my own she is fine. I think she needs time to calm down after the upset of D turning up again.

27.6.03
Got a deep cut to her right front paw in the garden. Cleaned and bandaged.
29.6.03
Cut appears to be healing but still hobbling around.
3.7.03
Rang Emma about continual tail chasing. She said it was probably stress caused by the re – emergence of D. Continue with therapy and report in two weeks.
19.7.03
Worse than ever at Mums so it's back to the drawing board.
3.8.03
Appointment with Emma. She insisted it was still attention seeking but really thought Laurel also needed drug support (for Laurel not me!) so gave her a course of Clomicalm and asked to report back in a month.
8.8.03
Appears to be improving slightly.
24.8.03
Over the past few weeks she seems up and down. Here on my own she seems very anxious. Bad if anyone comes to visit. Still taking Clomicalm.
7.12.03
Another appointment with Emma. She appears to have run out of ideas. She even suggested getting another dog!

At this stage I noticed another part of Laurel's behaviour manifest itself. She was now growling while chasing her tail and although I was certain this was not aggression it must have looked pretty nasty to anybody that didn't know her. If your hand or foot happened to be in the vicinity of her tail she would attack her tail but make no move whatsoever towards the hand or foot. Try telling that to a stranger. She was getting to be the same while on her lead. If there were any other dog around while she was on her lead she would growl and snarl attempting to reach the other animal. If, however she was not attached to a lead as the dog walked by she would give a wary glance but carry on her way. After a short walk in the nearby woodland Laurel and I returned home only to find Ray, my neighbour working in his front garden with Scrumpy, his greyhound wondering around aimlessly. Scrumpy (His owner, Christine was rather partial to the odd can of Scrumpy cider – hence the name) was so placid, and I often stopped to make a fuss of him. On this particular day as we approached the house, Laurel caught sight of him and being attached to her lead went into her aggressive performance. Scrumpy completely ignored her. As we got closer the growling became more and more fierce but at no stage concerned me. I knew Laurel too well. When we reached the house Laurel was in full flow and when Ray saw what was happening he looked very concerned. I stopped and said to Ray "watch this", and unclipped Laurel's lead so she was now free to do whatever she liked and there was nothing between Laurel or Scrumpy. I saw Ray's jaw hit the floor. Laurel slowly walked to my back gate and waited for me to let her in. Ray couldn't believe what he had just seen. This may have been a show of protection for me as she had done with Billy the English bull terrier the years previous. I knew Scrumpy well and Laurel even better so I knew no problems would occur. Ray often spoke about this incident and has said he was convinced Laurel was about to attack – just like the time Laurel got into his car as he was leaving for work. Ray had started his car just as I opened my front door and as Ray hadn't closed his car door Laurel was in there on top of him. All I saw was a mass of paperwork flying in the air and Laurel going round and round Ray's neck licking his face and whacking him in the eye with her tail. I dare say it wasn't half as funny for Ray as it was for me. After much apologising Laurel was forgiven.

Over the months with constant work on the tail chasing behavioural problem Laurel became a lot better but even as I write some 3 - 4 years after it all began she still, on occasions feels the need to chase her tail. She always appears fine when she is on her own with someone but with more than one person around she spins around biting her tail. I have come to the conclusion that this is as good as it gets and after discussing this with Geoffrey, he is in agreement. In fact, it was only recently that Geoffrey informed me of the concerns for Laurel's behaviour at the time. At one of the practice meetings attended by Emma and Geoffrey they only gave Laurel a 50/50 chance of making any sort of recovery, as this was one of the worst cases they had seen. He also said it as purely down to the dedication, patience, love and damned hard work by people around Laurel (myself and more so my parents) that contributed to her being as good as was.

To this day I have to confess I don't understand this behavioural problem. Take this example. If there is more than one person including myself in, say, the lounge, watching television. Laurel will sit by my side chasing her tail vying for my attention. I ignore her – she carries on tail chasing. She stops so I go to her to make a fuss of her thus rewarding her for not chasing her tail. She immediately chases her tail again so I ignore her again. After she has worked so hard to get my attention she then does something that she knows will be ignored. This truly is the strangest behaviour I, or anyone I have spoken to, have ever come across and sadly I think I know where most of it may have stemmed from. This was also not to be the worst of Laurel's problems.

Two buddies together.

Laurel doing a spot of sunbathing.

CHAPTER NINETEEN

STARTING OVER

Laurel's behaviour continued to progress slowly but soon reached a stage where it just was not going to improve anymore. It had to be accepted by all concerned she would improve no more and there would always be that element of attention seeking from her. Laurel, Harri and me continued living at Drayton quite happily with, thankfully no more visits from Debbie.

Towards the end of that year whilst visiting a small local paper shop in Drayton village I bumped into someone I had not seen for over twenty years.

Back in 1977 I met and got engaged to a lovely girl called Christine. My first real love you could say. Although we were very young, for several years we were inseparable. I would spend most weekends at Christine's parents house and we would meet each other a couple of times during the week – Christine's homework permitting. Christine's parent's, John and Doreen were and still are wonderful people who always did show me lots of love and kindness. Her brother Paul who was then about twelve was always good for a laugh so at that time I was very happy – in fact they really were my second family. I always admired John's keenness to do jobs around the house whenever he had the time. He worked five and half days a week as a company director (that's without work he undoubtedly brought home with him) and for the other day and a half in the week he was always doing some project around the house or in the garden.

When I turned seventeen in May 1978 I had my first driving lesson from John. I remember it as if it were yesterday. He took me out in Doreen's metallic green Vauxhall Viva to a small-disused airfield just outside Norwich and taught me the basics of accelerator, clutch and brake control. For the next hour or so there we were going up and down this airfield. Looking back it must have driven poor John bonkers but for me it was real excitement. When it was time to leave for home I drove most of the way home but did not have the confidence to drive over what was then a very narrow bridge where they lived in Taverham. Had I have conquered the bridge I would still have had to master the turn into their drive, which, even by today's standards is a bit tricky. This outing put me in very good stead for the next week when I had my first 'professional' driving lesson. Over the next few months with lessons from my instructor and John and Doreen I took my driving test on 18th October 1978 and passed first time. After taking only 10 professional lessons most of the credit has to go to both John and Doreen for my pass and for that I will always be grateful.

I had been saving hard for my first car and it wasn't too long before it arrived. A purple 1969 Ford Escort registration number TYS 435G bought for £345.00 cash. For the next couple of months John put in hours of work restoring various parts on the car. Tins of body filler for the smaller jobs, replacing floor panels, boot panels, front wings and engine tuning ensued and every single job carried out by John was done to perfection. The same is

130

true of him today. If ever the saying "If a jobs worth doing, it's worth doing well" should be applied to anybody, it's John Woods. I was with John as helper for most of the evenings but at only seventeen my knowledge was limited so I could only really do the menial tasks. Working with John, however gave me immense satisfaction because I always knew the end product would look just great. John even took on the job of re-spraying parts of the car – at the expense of Doreen's cooking. As the garage adjoined the house, invisible particles of purple spray paint found their way in somehow. All the skirting in the house had a purple tinge to it and everything poor Doreen cooked – normally a fabulous cook - tasted as if it had been swept up from a car re-spray floor. The finished car was fantastic. It reminded me a bit of the movie 'Chitty Chitty Bang Bang'. The bit at the start of the film when Professor Potts takes a mangled piece of metal into his workshop and days later he drives out a beautiful motorcar. John had taken this average looking vehicle into his garage and a couple of months later a fabulous, gleaming Mark 1 Ford Escort appeared. I had my first car and was so proud of it and so indebted to John for the many hours he had put into it for me.

Christine and me were very happy. Unfortunately, as time passed I began to realise there were other people around other than Christine and I began enjoying time around my drinking mates and spending time at nightclubs rather than with her. The inevitable happened and Christine and me split. My son Steven was born but that was not the reason for us splitting as we continued seeing each other for a while after this happened. Looking back now Christine must truly have been a special person to have found it in her heart to forgive me for such an action even though we split shortly afterwards. There was no big falling out, no big argument just an ending. I still loved her and I knew she still loved me but there was a big wide world out there and I wanted to see some of it. What would have happened had we stayed together – who knows?

Towards the end of 2000 I walked out of our local paper shop towards my car in the car park when a voice behind me said " I'd recognise that walk anywhere!" When I turned round it was Doreen. She always did say that I had a very distinctive walk. As I stood talking to Doreen, enquiring about John, Paul and Christine a young girl about 10 years old appeared obviously with Doreen. It took me about two seconds to realise it must have been Christine's daughter. We had a chat about old times as we walked towards Doreen's car where John was sitting. It was great talking to them both again. Apparently Christine was living a couple of miles away from me at a place called Thorpe Marriott. For twenty or more years I had not set eyes on Christine even though I was later to find out that on two occasions we had lived a stones throw away from each other. John, Doreen, Emma (Christine's daughter) and myself, said our goodbyes and I was on my way. It was a really pleasant meeting.

That Christmas I decided to send my surrogate Mum and Dad a Christmas card and I was so pleased to receive a New Year card in return but in all essence I didn't think I would see them again, after all it was over twenty years since I had last seen them so by my calculation I would be in my sixties the next time we met.

132

Shortly after Christmas, feeling a little board one Saturday afternoon I decided to take a walk down to my local The Red Lion in Drayton. After spending a good part of the afternoon and early evening there, at around eight o'clock I thought it time I started the walk home. After saying my goodbyes I headed for the door and as I went to open it I noticed, out of the corner of my eye, a couple coming into the pub through the same door. I took a step to the side to allow them to come in first. It was really using peripheral vision as I couldn't tell you what the couple looked like or what they were wearing - that is until the female of the couple caught hold of my arm. It was Christine. After all this time there she was in front of me. The chap she was with carried on walking to the bar obviously not wanting to socialise so Christine and I continued our conversation. We went over the old times and asked about each other's families and it transpired that Christine's husband had left her for another woman when Christine was six months pregnant with Emma. When she told me that I just wanted to cuddle her but thought better of it. It was then Christine dropped a bit of a bombshell. "We'll have to go out for a drink sometime" she said. I couldn't believe my luck so I told her my phone number (about a dozen times) very slowly and deliberately and asked her to call me. We said our goodbyes and I left thinking 'what a coincidence that was. As I walked towards home I began thinking to myself. Something on the lines of: ' now I know I've had more than a few beers but that did really happen just then didn't it?' Just as an after thought I began wondering who the fella was. I knew Christine would never cheat on anybody but all of this was very strange. I walked home that night with a beaming smile on my face hoping Christine would phone me.

133

Laurel was there waiting for me at home and after the usual manic greeting from her we both settled down for the evening. She really was worth coming home to.

The following week I received the call and Christine and I arranged an evening out together. When we sat down in the Cellar House pub on the outskirts of Norwich it felt to both of us that the previous twenty years or so hadn't happened. It felt so natural being together again even if it was for only a drink and a chat. We went over old times and filled each other in on recent happenings to us both. The chap that Christine had been with on the night I had bumped into her was her then boyfriend. This relationship, I was to learn later was flagging badly and it was only going to be a matter of time before it ended. Maybe the reappearance of me made it end slightly sooner than it would have done but basically it was dead anyway. With me 'free and single' (I did omit the word 'young') the most natural course in the world to take was for me and Christine to start over again, which was precisely what we did.

Needless to say both sets of parents were ecstatic with our news as was Christine's daughter Emma. Emma and I hit it off from day one. In many ways – the bad ways some would say – she is a lot like me, which I do take as a compliment because in my eyes she was and is a wonderful child.

Before too long, myself, Christine and Emma were making plans to buy our own home – along with Laurel, Harri and Christine's West Highland Terrier dog, Rosie. We all realised this would be the real test for Laurel.

134

My son Steven on one of his visits having a lay in –
until Laurel appeared, that is.

CHAPTER TWENTY

P.A.C.T.

Christine and Laurel's first meeting was hilarious as was Laurel's first meeting with just about everyone. I remember and instance when at the vets when an elderly woman came in and seeing Laurel's tail wagging frantically and her trying desperately to reach her the lady asked if it was alright to make a fuss of her. After assuring her there was no problem the lady bent down to see her. Laurel went mad as usual. The lady loved every moment of it and stayed with Laurel for about five minutes. You would have thought this person was Laurel's long lost owner. It was then I said to the lady "Does this dog belong to you?" She smiled and said, "I wish she did".

Christine and Emma's first introduction to Laurel was much the same. They were obviously both used to their own dog Rosie who was - and indeed still is a lovely placid dog. When I first met Rosie at Christine's house, Rosie came to the door barking initially, but upon seeing me she went flat on her back with all fours in the air – to which my comment was "What a tart". I wasn't sure if I had had this effect on her or if this was a regular occurrence. Upon Christine and Emma's arrival at my house I thought it best to shut Laurel away until everyone was settled – more so Laurel. When she did eventually meet them both the inevitable happened – she went mad. Emma went to the floor to meet Laurel – wrong move when you have long, flowing, blond hair. The hair was an easy target and through all the excitement Laurel had mouthfuls of Emma's hair. Christine laughing hysterically made this worse. There was Laurel on top of poor Emma who was trying to get up but unable to through laughter. A memorable first meeting. In fact this type of "attack" (I use that term very loosely) from Laurel now has it's own title compliments of Christine. Whenever this happens now, we say 'you have been Laurelled'. It was pretty obvious to me there would be no problems as far as our animals were concerned although they still had to meet each other. The one slight downside is that Emma is allergic to cats so although she loves making a fuss of Harri, she has to remember to wash her hands before she touches her face or a terrible rash will appear.

It was around this time that I took to doing some volunteer work at an animal sanctuary a few miles outside Norwich at a place called Hingham. This all came about after I picked up a leaflet whilst making a small donation to P.A.C.T. at a Sunday market. PACT stands for People For Animal Care Trust. After reading the leaflet I decided now would be a perfect time to give some of my time to other animals less fortunate than my own. Christine and myself hadn't found our dream home at that time but were still looking hard so I had no work on that front and I wasn't about to do major work on my own home as I knew I wouldn't be there for much longer. This left me with some spare time even if only until we found our new home.

After telephoning I took my first trip out to PACT and upon arrival realised how desperately they needed help, both financially and manually. The place was run down but everybody there was determined to help the animals and for that they have my utmost respect. George and Chris the founders work tirelessly, raising funds in anyway they can. I was introduced to one of the few full time workers there, Neil who began by showing me around the place. As it was a lovely sunny day being out in the open with animals from pot bellied pigs, ducks, cats dogs, and horses was my idea of paradise – if only Laurel could see this. Neil took me through various routines like feeding the horses and goats before taking me to the dog pens. One dog immediately caught my eye. A massive Rottweiler looking so ferocious, barking at the fence of her pen and frantically was trying to get over the top of it. When I asked Neil about her he explained she would probably never leave because of her manner. She was fine with people she knew but not with people she didn't. When I asked if it was all noise (like Laurel) he assured me it wasn't and she would (in his words) tear your head off! I wasn't convinced and more encounters with this beast were to follow.

After being introduced to some of the other animals I took a couple of the dogs around the adjoining field for their daily walk. One that I remember very well was a little Staffie named Bo. He had been brought in because he was too much of a handful for his owners and had become vicious and "attacked one of them". It later transpired that he had growled at one of his owners when they took food away from him. I'll let you make your own mind up on that one. I, myself never saw any aggressive tendencies in him in the many times I took him for walks over the coming months and he was eventually re-homed and is now very happy. Everytime I was with him I wanted to bring him home myself. Having said that, if I had carried that out with all the animals I felt that way toward I would have to find a bigger house and I fear, a new wife to be. Bo was exceptional on a lead especially for a Staffie who are renowned for wanting to go where they want in the shortest possible time. Bo never pulled at all and the lead always hung loose as we walked. He had to wear a muzzle as he was not keen on other animals especially cats so a precautionary measure had to be taken. He, like most Staffies I know was full of energy and his highlight of the day was his walk around the field and I must say it gave me as much pleasure to see him happy.

After discussing with Neil that it was possible for me to do a couple of mornings a week I was told I could turn up when I liked as they would always have something to do for me. That was my first eventful morning at the PACT Animal Sanctuary. I did, however leave feeling a little guilty I hadn't done more and the fact that a lot of these animals were desperate for a loving home. The one consolation I did have was that, without PACT who knows where the animals would be. Abandoned, killed, in the wild – who knows? At least at PACT they were given a second chance and with the limited finances and ability they were extremely well cared for.

Over the next few months I managed to give the animals at PACT, one, sometimes two mornings a week and my visits rarely went by without incident. On one occasion I arrived just as the dogs were being led one by one from the sleeping areas to the outdoor pens. Some of the more untrustworthy dogs had to be taken by the full time workers, as they were familiar faces. One such dog was being lead by Neil was the big Rottweiler I had seen previously. Upon seeing me, Neil called me over as he sat down with the dog on a tree stump. The dog was muzzled for obvious reasons but still very intimidating. As I approached I couldn't believe the size of her paws – they were like human hands. She began barking and snarling as I approached and had to be physically restrained by Neil. " Come and meet Chrissie," said Neil. I had to laugh because that was the name of my partner at home, whom I was sure would see the funny side of being likened to a Rottweiler. As I approached I crouched down, talking to Chrissie all the time. The barking stopped and I was encouraged by Neil to coax the back of Chrissie's head, which I did very slowly. She seemed calm until I looked her in the eye. It was like a scene from the Omen – her look changed immediately. Her eyes changed and I said to Neil " she's gonna go". He tightened his grip on the lead and Chrissie went straight for my head. Luckily Neil had a firm grip and her head stopped about two inches from mine. I didn't move an inch. By this time she was barking and growling trying to reach me. Neil said, " You're very brave not moving and you have shown her you're not scared." "Are you joking?" I said "I'm shitting myself here!" I think I stayed where I was out of fear more than bravery. After calming her down Neil took her to her pen and told me she would soon get used to me and the trust would grow. I wasn't finished with Chrissie by a long way.

After one particular visit to PACT with the usual dog walking and a little 'mucking out' of some of their pens, I decided to pay Chrissie a visit in her pen before I left. This time alone. As there had been a complaint from one of the neighbours about the dog barking the pens were erected a little way from the other animals to help keep the dogs calm. There must be a dozen or so wire-netting pens with an open 'corridor' walkway that goes through the middle. This is really the 'double lock' so should a dog do his or

141

her Steve McQueen impersonation from the Great Escape they would only get as far as the open corridor which is also locked at either end. After entering the walkway I made my way to where Chrissie was. She was already barking and this time she really did look like a wild dog. As I got to her pen she was literally taking off in an attempt to clear the fence and get to me, which I must admit was a little worrying. The pens themselves stand approximately eight foot high and her massive front paws were almost reaching the top. I began to speak to her very calmly and almost immediately she stopped barking. I got into a crouched position and produced a small dog biscuit from my pocket which Chrissie immediately caught sight of. There we were about a foot away from each other albeit separated by a fence, staring at each other with me talking to her all the time. I then decided to try something. I said 'SIT!' very sternly with an immediate response of her plonking her backside on the concrete. 'Give me your paw' was the next command and up came he left paw. This proved to me that somewhere along the line she had had some form of training. I gently touched her paw through the netting and handed her the biscuit, which she took with the gentleness of a baby. Once finished she looked for more and upon realising there was no more we just sat there staring at each other. Just like our first meeting something then changed. The look in her eye changed to the beast from the Omen and without warning she took of against the netting level with my head, snarling in the process. Again I didn't flinch but instead kept talking to her calmly. " You don't frighten me at all" I lied, hoping and praying the fence was strong enough to hold her solid frame.

I left PACT that day with the knowledge that I had made some headway with Chrissie and that pleased me no-end. I was now even more determined for her to gain trust in me so I could maybe take her for walks. The way I saw it was, if she was never going to taste the freedom of being in a loving family, she could at least taste the freedom with the kind people inside the boundaries of PACT. Sadly for reasons other than her manner this was not be.

Later that year Christine and myself found the home we had been looking for and just like any new home there was work to be done to put our own mark on it. Although it was in good order generally, we still had lots to do in the decorating department and in the garden. All in all this meant I would be tied up with my own duties and would not be able to offer PACT much time until we were settled. I explained this to Neil who was more than understanding and said I could go to help out whenever I had any spare time. Although I still supported PACT through sponsorship and donations – both financially and donating goods to the shops they now run to raise money – I just didn't have any spare time of my own to visit them to help out, hands on.

Only recently, however, I did pay a visit on one of Pact's 'open days' when the general public can visit to find out more about the place and take part in the fun day to help raise money for the animals. Christine, Emma, my parents and myself took a drive out one Sunday afternoon. As we entered I saw Neil and my first question was "how's Chrissie?" What he told me brought a massive lump to my throat but also made me happy. Shortly after I had stopped going to PACT it was discovered Chrissie had a serious stomach problem that turned out to be inoperable. There was, however, a gentleman that regularly visited Pact who owned a great deal of land and knowing Chrissies position offered to take her so she could spend her last days in freedom. This she did. I could just imagine her running free in the open air, doing all the things our own well cared for dogs do. This made me happy. Sadly, Chrissie died about six months after she left PACT but I am sure she died a happy dog. One really sad thing is that I never got to take her for that walk I had promised her.

I am hoping to return to help out at PACT one day soon as I am sure there are many more Chrissie's and Bo's out there that all need just a little kindness.

CHAPTER TWENTY ONE

NEW HOME, NEW FAMILY.

Christine discovered our new home whilst looking through our local paper and I made a passing visit to the property when I finished work one summer morning – about 5.45 a.m. I liked what I saw very much and after a few viewings and one or two problems selling our own properties we bought it, and with help from both families we moved in just before Christmas 2001.

The property is a lovely 4 bed-roomed detached house but the real selling point for me (apart from the extremely large garden) was, about twenty feet from our front door is a massive field, which we are part owners of. Across the field is a small bridge that leads straight to the river Wensum. This had 'Laurel's field MK2' written all over it. Christine and I both fell in love with the whole set up and couldn't wait to get our own use out of it. It is so peaceful and quiet at anytime of day and Laurel and myself spend a great deal of time just walking by the river and around the field.

We decided to let Harri settle in to her new home before we introduced the two dogs which meant Laurel having an extended holiday at my parents and Rosie staying with Christine's Mum and Dad. We needed to keep Harri indoors to allow her to familiarise herself with the new surroundings. I installed a cat – flap in the back door and within a week or so she was out exploring her new territory. Although the large field existed across from our front door and the side of the house has boundaries with farmland she still only seemed to venture as far as her own garden discovering all the suntraps and sheltered places she needed to – that's when she was not sleeping on top of the boiler in our utility room. She is exactly the same today, always there to greet me whenever she hears the back door opening or my car in the driveway. The first thing I hear is her little bell on her collar, then her familiar little face appears from under one of the conifer trees or behind the greenhouse or some new hideaway she has discovered. As soon as she realises it's me it's the one hundred metres sprint towards me. It was quite funny on one particular day when Christine went out of the back door and heard Harri's bell in the distance, followed by the dash towards her. On realising it was Christine, however, she stopped almost dead in her tracks, turned around and wandered, slowly back to where she had come from. Christine found this highly amusing.

The decision to introduce the two dogs at the same time was taken so none of them would feel they were protecting their own territory and after Harri had settled in it was time for the dogs to move into their new home and be with their new family. We always knew there was going to be a problem with Rosie and Harri because the simple fact was Rosie hated cats and would give chase whenever possible. Harri had been used to a big bully of a dog for years so I knew it would be no problem for her but my real concerns were for Rosie. I was also concerned with how Laurel would react if another animal had a go at her 'sister' Harri. However, I was sure we could overcome these problems with a little patience and understanding.

146

One evening we introduced both dogs into their new home together and for the first few minutes everything was uneventful. Rosie was more concerned with Harri even though she couldn't see her as she was in the utility room. As I expected Harri didn't bother at all but just kept a safe distance on top of one of the units. It was a case of " I'm up here and you can't get me." Rosie was really bothered though and she lay by the utility room door with her nose pushed against the tiny gap at the bottom of the door. This was a little concerning as Rosie was really working herself into frenzy at the slightest noise Harri happened to make. Everything was fine until she barked and Laurel was on her like a ton of bricks, more from a defensive fear than out and out aggression. She pinned Rosie to the floor and as luck would have it, Rosie froze. I calmly (well as calmly as one can be when your dog has hold of another dog ready to attack) pulled Laurel away without saying a word. I didn't want to make matters even worse by showing the dogs I was concerned. Laurel never harmed her in any way and once again it was the noise factor that made it all sound worse than it really was. I realise if they were to live together one of them would have to be in charge but it was for them to sort out and me to make sure they didn't hurt each other. This episode really scared Rosie (and Christine) and I did feel for the poor mite although she was still so worked up over Harri. The rest of the evening was spent with the dogs basically keeping out of each other's way. Initially, Christine decided it would be best for Rosie to sleep in Emma's bedroom until she was settled. I knew Laurel would sleep wherever she lay so I set up her bed downstairs in the kitchen. Rosie was awake for most of the night, which in turn kept Emma awake, who in turn kept us awake. This was the first night after all. Things didn't change and Rosie just would not settle knowing there was a cat in the house and the slightest noise Harri made sent her crazy, which then alerted Laurel to a problem. Added to the fact that Emma was getting no sleep at all, Christine came to an agonising decision. She decided it would be better all round if Rosie stayed at her parent's full time. Having always owned Westies themselves, Christine's parents were only too happy to take her but all of this left me feeling a little sad. I really wanted everything to be perfect and I was sure – and I still am today – that with time and patience everything would have been fine. I fully appreciated Christine's concerns over the 'pinning' incident because I am the first to agree it didn't look very nice but it's a case of knowing and more importantly, trusting your own pet. I remember one day when I came home from work I walked into the lounge and sat on the floor with my back resting against the sofa. Immediately Laurel came to one side and lay down and soon after Rosie came to the other side and did the same. It was pure magic for me. As long as they were both treated equally I couldn't foresee a problem between them. I did agree with Christine's concerns over Rosie and Harri, however. It wasn't that we were worried what Rosie would do to her because she was nowhere near fast enough to catch her but it was the frenzy she got herself into when she knew Harri was around. With Rosie having slight breathing problems the condition she got herself into made her breathing worse so I couldn't help but reluctantly agree with Christine and her reasoning behind Rosie going to her parents. Much to our sadness Rosie made her move and although she is not in the best of health as I write, she is very happy and we see her often.

On another occasion Christine's brother Paul paid us a visit bringing his beautiful white Samoyed dog Sheena along. Once again we had to make certain she never came into contact with Harri as she was another one that didn't like our feline friends and given half a chance would probably have chased Harri for miles. Whilst Harri was in her bed, asleep in the utility room we took Sheena and Laurel out into the back garden with a couple of tennis balls and for a few moments everything was fine. This changed as soon as Sheena came a little close to me and Laurel launched herself at her and pinned her to the ground staring at her in the process. There was Laurel on top of a dog that was almost three times the size of her. Once again no harm was done but the warning shots were well and truly fired. Paul was mortified but both dogs continued playing with the ball. In fact it was then Laurel who backed off. From that day, sadly Laurel has been kept away from Rosie and Sheena. While this does sadden me I would never forgive myself should anything happen to any of the dogs through Laurel's own fear and her protection of me. The only times I have ever seen her carry out these sort of actions is when she is either protecting me or she is fearing for her own safety. I really do not believe she is a naturally aggressive dog as has been proved many times when we are out walking. If other peoples dogs leave Laurel alone she will certainly not bother them but take the easier option of walking by. That is not the actions of a dog that wants to fight.

Little Rosie. ("Rodo" as she is often called)

CHAPTER TWENTY TWO

FUNNY LITTLE WAYS.

We all settled into our new home fairly quickly and both Harri and Laurel seemed very happy. I was extremely pleased with the relationship Christine was building with Laurel. Although initially she was a little scared of her because of all the growling noises she made when play fighting with me, she soon realised she was totally harmless – even bordering on being a bit of a wimp. I continued doing decorating that was required and also making our new garden into something to be proud of. As the garden stood it had nothing in it at all apart from being surrounded by conifer trees that stood about twenty feet tall. This blocked an immense amount of light and also was not at all good for security. I began by removing half of the trees and replaced them with fencing which actually made you feel you were outside and not still in a room when walking into the garden. I changed various parts in the garden, erecting a hexagonal greenhouse (with help from my Dad), moving the summerhouse into a sunny corner and installing various seating areas for summer sun and summer shade. Once these tasks were completed and Christine began stocking up with plants the garden really took shape and although still not fully complete it is a lovely place to spend time in through the summer months for both animals and humans alike.

As we all spent more and more time together we all had to get used to each others different ways and both

Christine and Emma were not only getting used to my funny little ways but also Laurel and Harri's as well. One of the things that still has Christine in fits of laughter even today is Laurel's response to the word ' bucket'. A harmless noun one may think but if said in the presence of Laurel it sends her into a mad frenzy. Her tail will be rigid, the fur on her back will be on end and she will be running around barking. I have absolutely no idea when this started or where it originated. The one thing I have noticed is when she does try to bite a bucket outside; she finds it impossible to keep it still thus ending up chasing it half way round the garden. Laurel can be in any frame of mind, eating, sleeping, playing but if she hears the mention of the word ' bucket' she goes crazy looking for it. If the word is said outside she goes straight to the shed where she knows one is kept. Christine and I tried a little experiment one evening when Laurel was sleeping. We spoke at the same volume level as normal but a couple of times in the middle of a sentence I would throw in the word ' bucket'. Laurel's ears pricked up immediately but as I carried on my conversation she slowly drifted back to sleep. Again I put ' bucket' into the conversation and this time she was up, off her chair and barking at the door. Attention seeking – maybe. Funny to watch – most definitely. Christine was in hysterics.

Something happened on one occasion when I was attempting some DIY that really made me laugh. Anyone that knows me well will know that with something's I have the patience of a saint – like training and caring for animals for instance but in other ways I am the first to admit I was at the back of the queue when patience was handed out. On this particular day things were not going too well on the DIY front and as there was no-one in the house apart from Laurel and me I let fire with a few expletives, one of them being 'oh f*** it'. Laurel went crazy which made me think my anger had upset her but I soon realised what had set her off. She had mistakenly thought I had said 'bucket'. After realising this the anger concerning the DIY disappeared as I was in stitches over what she had thought I'd said.

I still find it incredible how animals can associate with so many different words and Laurel is certainly no exception. When she first began staying at my parents while I was doing my two day shifts I often used to refer to it as 'going up to nanny's' (referring to my Mum) and now as soon as the word 'nanny' is mentioned she is up and almost waiting at the back door for my parents to arrive. Although Christine works part-time I decided to still allow Laurel to stay at my parent's for my two-day shifts for their benefit as much as Laurels. My Mum and Dad both Love her to pieces and I know she has brought so much happiness into their lives. In fact my Mum has often said she could think no more of her if she was her Grandchild.

Another little trait Laurel has is to constantly stare at me when she lies on her chair in the evening. I will be sat on the other side of the room and I can see her out of the corner of my eye staring. As I turn to talk to her, her tail wags and she wiggles around like a worm. I can then put her into what Christine refers to as a hypnotic trance. All I do is look toward her and say very slowly "go to sleep, go to sleep, go to sleep" and slowly her eyes lids drop as though she is being hypnotised. This is also a funny sight to see and I have never quite been able to send her fully to sleep as I begin laughing.

Laurel was also very keen to "help" with the gardening particularly when she had a tennis ball with her. Whatever you decided to do, be it raking, sweeping, digging or planting the ball was always dropped in front of you in such a way that you cannot continue without moving it. The more you move it the more it comes back. It's quite funny when Christine and I are in the garden together but in different areas. Christine maybe planting at one end and I maybe raking at the other. This posses a real dilemma for Laurel. Firstly she would come to me and drop the ball, which I would then pick up and say, "Go and see Christine". Laurel would then race to where Christine was working and then the cry would be " No! Take it to your Dad" at which point Laurel comes running back to me. This can go on for ages and it's not Laurel that tires first. I once read an article that stated that we humans think we train a dog to go a fetch a ball when we throw it but in fact it's the dog that trains us to throw the ball when they bring it back to us. Enough said I think.

We also had the huge, inviting field opposite our front door to explore and it didn't take long before Laurel and me were wondering down by the river together. We'd walk across the road with her tennis ball and as we walked through the half dozen trees onto the main part of the field Laurel would always run to the right side of the field toward a wooden bench on the boundary. She knew I would head for the bench where I would sit for a while throwing her ball for her to retrieve. She absolutely loved this activity and would run for hours never seeming to tire. After this we would head toward the river walking around

154

a fenced paddock. The river is actually separated from the field by a dyke about seven or eight feet wide. At one section of the field there is a wooden bridge over the dyke but I never allow Laurel to use that unless I can carry her across it. The wooden bridge is slatted with gaps of about two inches between the slats. In fact they are just big enough for a dog to get its paw trapped in. Should the animal in question be moving quickly or even running at the time, it's leg would snap like a stick. Laurel soon got used to the idea of not using the wooden bridge and made no attempt to cross the dyke using it. The other place to cross the dyke was a little further down the field where there were two solid steel walkways. The walkways are about two foot wide and made of steel chequer plate material with no handrails. They both ran parallel to each other about four feet apart. This was always our route to the river. On one particular day Laurel was in front of me doing her own thing but always making sure I was not far behind when she came to the two steel bridges. Normally she will wait for me to catch up before she crosses the dyke but on this day she had other ideas. She stepped onto one of the steel bridges and began crossing. Upon realising I was not with her she turned to see where I was, carrying on walking as she did so. Suddenly she walked straight over the edge into the dyke and completely under the water. By this time I was only a few yards away and was quickly onto the bridge. I knelt down, put my arm into the water and managed to feel her collar. With a swift yank I pulled her headfirst onto the bridge. The look of horror on her face said it all. If she could have spoken I'm sure it would have been something on the lines of " What the hell happened there?" I couldn't stop laughing and Laurels actions made the incident even funnier. There was I sitting on the floor laughing at what I had just seen and there was Laurel jumping all over me barking and play biting almost as though she saw the funny side of it too. I have no doubt had I not been around Laurel would have pulled herself free but it certainly made me aware of just how deep the dyke actually was. Needless to say Laurel always has eyes front whenever she crosses the bridge now.

We have and indeed still do spend many happy hours on Laurel's field and we all consider ourselves very lucky to be situated in such a beautiful location. Sadly for reasons I shall come onto later, Laurel's exercise on her field has had to be drastically cut.

A frosty morning on Laurel's 'new' field.

CHAPTER TWENTY-THREE

A SAD DISCOVERY.

During 2002 Christine and me continued working on our home to make it a nice family home with continuing help from Laurel when working in the garden.

After one of Laurel's weekly trips to my parents, my Mum pointed out that she was concerned with Laurel's right eye which appeared very watery and a little swollen. Her 'third' eyelid was constantly coming down to cover the eye so I knew there was a problem and after bathing it I decided a trip to the vets would be necessary. Once again, Laurel was extremely excited to go there – strange dog. When Geoffrey put a special dye into Laurel's eye it was quite easy to see some scar tissue in there even with the naked eye. Something very sharp had sliced her eye and an abscess had formed as part of the healing process. This 'something very sharp' was almost certainly a cat's claw. Whilst at my parent's house an unknown cat had appeared at the bottom of the garden walking along the top of the fence. As soon as Laurel saw it she did the usual trick of bounding toward it to see if it would run away. This one, however, stayed put and stared down at Laurel a couple of feet out of reach. Laurel, of course was frantically trying to get to it, barking madly in the process. As the cat walked along the fence with that familiar "you can't get me" kind of look, it stumbled and fell into my parent's garden with Laurel eagerly waiting to pounce. Apparently it was all over in a matter of seconds as the cat hit the floor and was back on top of the fence virtually without touching the ground. In the melee, however, the cat must have lashed out with its claws and caught Laurel in the eye. The cat wandered off and Laurel came trundling in with the "I sorted that one out" look on her face but not 'sorting it' as well as she thought.

Obviously we had to watch for infection in her eye and she was given a course of eye drops. I was asked to report back the next week when Geoffrey was satisfied all was well and the eye was healing nicely. The injury didn't look very nice and had obviously given her a great deal of discomfort but it could have been much worse. I entered all the details in Laurel's reference book and upon reading this prior to starting this book some of my entries amused me. This is what I had written concerning her eye injury:

10.10.02
Seems to be improving
16.10.03
Back to vets for check-up. He said it was definitely healing. Keep applying drops for one more week and everything should be fine.

26.10.03
Laurel now back to 'normal' HELP!

Later that year I began noticing another problem manifesting itself this time with her back legs. Ever since she was a tiny puppy she had so much energy and when on her walks she would run and run for miles with no ill effect on her whatsoever. What I began noticing was, after a walk when she had crashed out in her bed, she really

160

struggled to walk when getting up again. It was almost as if she had pulled a muscle in her back legs, her right leg being the worst of the two. At first I thought nothing of it and brushed it off as her over exerting herself and the fact that although she was only six, she was getting a little older. She never appeared in any discomfort when chasing her ball on the field but only when she stopped running. We continued our routine of exercise with both myself and my parents monitoring the situation concerning her legs. Some days she was fine and others she was struggling to stand up straight. The final straw for me was when I watched her eat her food one evening. With her head buried in the food bowl I noticed her trying to lift her right back leg off the floor and then very gingerly placing it back on the floor only to try to lift the other leg up. This continued until she finished her food and went to lie in her bed. I realised she must have been in some sort of discomfort but in contradiction to that she was fine when running around the field. As a precautionary measure I decided to take her to see Geoffrey for his opinion on the issue.

On December 27th 2002 after Laurel causing the usual commotion in the vet surgery waiting room we went in to see Geoffrey and I explained the problem Laurel was having with her back legs. After watching Laurel wander around the room Geoffrey noticed that both her rear legs were twisting in slightly – something I thought she had always done and it was perfectly natural. This wasn't the case and it wasn't a natural manoeuvre at all and it signified this was the only way she could walk with any sort of comfort so something was seriously wrong. After a closer examination, Geoffrey felt all around her knee joints feeling no obvious problems with them or her ligaments and more importantly, not appearing to give Laurel any discomfort in the process. It was decided that she would have a course of anti–inflammatory tablets to see if they had any effect. Geoffrey also pointed out that no matter what sort of pain she was potentially in she would still go crazy on the field more from adrenalin than anything else. When the word "field" was mentioned she would be up and running within seconds when minutes before she could hardly walk. This was just pure excitement, I was told and she would only really suffer when the excitement wore off. This all seemed to add up and make perfect sense. I made an appointment for a re-visit and began her on her course of medication. The course of tablets given to Laurel appeared to have very little effect on her back leg movement. It was truly heartbreaking to see her get up from her bed in the mornings, her whole back end twisted and contorted. I knew deep down we had a serious problem. She was now also having problems getting onto her chair in the evening. She would approach her chair – one that previously she would jump on with no effort at all – and lay her head on the edge of it, almost as if she were weighing up the height of it. She would then take two or three steps back just as a penalty taker does on the football field, and then run at the chair. Sometimes, first time she would take off and land exactly in the desired position on the chair. Other times, however, her rear legs did not have enough power in them and she would fall head first into the chair, which was such a sad sight to see. On other occasions she would make her run only to stop at the last minute to re-adjust and have another go. She'd back up again then go for it one more time. I have watched her attempt this two or three times before she perfected her manoeuvre. On other occasions I have gone behind her to help lift her on her chair but she appears to get angry at this so I try to let her do it herself. It's almost as if she is too proud to admit she needs help to get on her chair.

For much of the time during this very worrying period, Laurel seemed a very sad dog – something I had not seen in her before. Although she did her best to play and go for walks, she always crashed out and looked in so much pain when she tried to get up again.

On the 6th January 2003 (Laurels birthday) I received some tragic news totally unconnected with Laurels predicament. One of my best friends died. Mick had been a friend for twenty years and like Graham, was more like a brother to me. The three of us shared so many happy, funny and sad times together. The banter between us all was as good as any comedy team on the television. We got on so well together and I can honestly say when Mick died, part of the team died to. We had all had a super time at Graham's house on New Years Eve, six days previous, but it was sadly the last time I saw my 'brother' Mick. He had come to collect me early on New Years Eve so we could go back to his house to have a pre-party party before we travelled on to Grahams.

One story I always tell about Mick is one I will share with you now and it could have easily been a sketch in Only Fools And Horses.

Mick was married four times and the split with his third wife turned very nasty. In fact she virtually emptied his home of its contents. Like she said at the time though, she had bought nearly everything but as Mick pointed out, with *his* money. After they split Mick decided he would go shopping for the essential things you need in a home – like sheets, pillows, an iron etc. (She had turned up one evening to collect some belongings when Mick was in the middle of ironing. Mick being Mick kept out of her way until she had gone but when he returned to finish his ironing she had taken the iron and the ironing board leaving the clothes on the floor.) Mick decided to enlist the help of his two best mates Laurel and Hardy – a.k.a. Graham and Steve to help him choose some of these household items so we travelled to Great Yarmouth on market day to pick up some things. Mick was one of those people that, if he was to buy something he would buy the first thing he saw, no matter if it was the best, the cheapest, or whatever. He just didn't like messing around from one shop to another trying to find one thing. When we reached the market place he decided to look for some pillows and a fitted sheet for his bed. The first pillows he came across were 99p each. They'll do said Mick and picked two up. Graham then pointed out; because of their quality he'd probably need about seven of them to hold his head up. Mick was undeterred. We then came to the fitted sheets. Once again he picked up the first pack he saw. "That'll do." I took the pack from him to see what he was about to buy. "You do realise this is for a king size bed don't you?" I said. "Yeh that'll be fine" said Mick. Graham then chirped in " Have you got a king size bed then?" to which Mick came out with the classic line " No but that won't matter – I'll tuck it in at the edges!" He was deadly serious. Graham and I looked at each other and creased up with laughter. That was Mick. There are so many funny stories involving Mick, Graham and myself – in fact enough to write another book.

164

Another day perhaps. He was a big man with an even bigger heart and I miss him dearly to this day.

Although Mick was ill and was waiting for a heart by-pass the shock I experienced when I received the telephone call from Graham equalled that of the one when I was told my Nan had left us. I remember Graham's words vividly. "Stevie, I got some bad news. I've just had a call from Julie (Mick's daughter) Mick's had a heart attack" At this point I thought Graham was about to say something like ' They've taken him to the University Hospital'. Graham went on " He died half an hour ago". I went numb with shock and could not even carry on talking to Graham. This was one of the saddest times of my life equalling the sad departure of my Nan and Granddad but I now had to turn my attentions to my main priority - to sort out Laurel's problems.

On the 14th January 2003 we returned to the vets for Laurel's x-rays to see if more light could be shed on the problem with her legs. Obviously animals don't tend to lie still for x-rays (especially dogs like Laurel) so a general anaesthetic was going to be needed whilst the x-rays were carried out. On our previous visit to see Geoffrey I had pointed out, what appeared to be a small fatty lump on Laurel's tummy and it was decided to remove this at the same time Laurel was anaesthetised to save her having to go through it all again. Leaving Laurel at the vets in the morning brought the memories back once again. Mum and Dad leaving me at the hospital, me leaving Laurel for her previous operation and of course, Mick's funeral – I knew the tears wouldn't be far away and they weren't long in coming.

165

Needless to say, the rest of the day seemed like a week with my thoughts going from Laurel to Mick and back to Laurel again. To say I was dreading the news from Geoffrey was an understatement even though at this stage the dreaded 'C' word hadn't been mentioned. After one of the longest days of my life had passed, my parents came to take me to the vets to collect Laurel and be told their findings. I needed someone to take me because I knew the state Laurel would be in after coming round from her anaesthetic. I also knew the state I would be in if the news was serious.

When I arrived at the surgery I sat in the waiting area for a short time before Geoffrey called me in to his room. I could tell by his manner and his look that all was not well. He began by telling me that the lump removed from Laurel's tummy was nothing more than a fatty lump as suspected. "Now for the bad news" was Geoffrey's next line. My heart sank like a lead balloon. He produced the X-rays saying this was one of the worst cases of arthritis he had seen in a dog of Laurel's age. He went on to tell me that if Laurel had been a twelve year old it would be classed as a serious case of arthritis so in a dog half that age it was severe. He pointed out the effected areas on the X-rays but as I had nothing to compare them with I could only take his word for it. Even I could see the miss – shaped bones though. He went on to tell me that she had probably had some pain from this for the past two years or so even though she had only just began to show it physically. I was devastated and the feeling of guilt was overwhelming. Was it something I had done? Was it something I hadn't done? Geoffrey assured me this had been completely out of my control and was more likely a hereditary complaint than

166

anything else. "Animals are very much like humans," Geoffrey said. "Some humans can go their whole life without seeing the inside of a doctors surgery or hospital whereas others are regular visitors due to genuine illnesses" I was beginning to think Laurel was falling into the latter category. Now we had established the problem we had to deal with it. She had been given an anti – inflammatory and pain killing injection while under sedation so when she came round she wouldn't be in any significant pain. Geoffrey prescribed Rimadyl anti – inflammatory and pain killing tablets so movement for Laurel wouldn't be as painful as it undoubtedly had been. I had to face the fact that Laurel would be on medication for the rest of her life. Her exercise had to be cut down to a minimum as well and this was one of the most difficult things to do with an energetic Staffie. Her mind was still as keen as ever to run for miles but her body was just not up to it anymore, even at the relatively young age of six. Obviously if the medication didn't work and the arthritis worsened I would then have to make the decision I was dreading but that was a bridge to cross if and when it appeared.

After a lengthy chat about the do's and don'ts for Laurel I returned to the reception area to collect my 'buddy'. She wandered out as she had done before after the previous operation all those years ago, although this time she was very sedated. Just seeing her in that condition broke my heart and she did her best to greet me the way she always had. Sadly the tail didn't wag and the eyes were drowsy but she still made a pull on her lead to get to me. As her sedation was making it difficult to walk I picked her up in my arms and the look in her eye just said "thanks". When

167

we got into my parents car she again tried to give the normal greeting but was too weak. With the sorry state she was in and the news I had just been told I cried. On the journey home Laurel lay in my arms just as she had when she was a few weeks old, like a small baby putting total trust in their parent. She slept for most of the journey. When we arrived home we all discussed our plan of action. We had to drastically cut down the exercise, make sure her medication was administered every day and also monitor her weight. Laurel has never been a large dog but the heavier she was, the more weight would go onto her arthritic legs.

Once again, I spent most of the night with Laurel in the lounge, only going to bed myself when I was sure she was ok and in a peaceful sleep herself.

At this stage I really began to wonder how long I would have Laurel for. Even though she was still very young I was not prepared to let her suffer in any way and watching her walking or trying to get on her chair was heartbreaking. Sometimes I would watch her sit down with her rear legs in some distorted but obviously comfortable position, in which she would then attempt to scratch herself. It was obvious she couldn't quite reach the spot because of the lack of free movement in her legs so I would have to go to her to help. I was sharing her pain with her. I questioned if there was any kind of operation for joint replacement available but was given a slow shake of the head from Geoffrey. The complaint was never going to go away and all I could really do was to try to suppress the pain by following Geoffrey's instructions and hoping and praying that she would be all right.

Laurel had to return to the vets in April 2003 because of eye problems. Something I can openly laugh about now but at the time was a little worrying. I had noticed on several occasions her eyes looked they were moving in different directions to one another, almost cross-eyed. Nothing too drastic, just a little bit out of alignment. Firstly I thought I was seeing things but began to notice it more often so with the 'better to be safe than sorry' attitude we returned to see Geoffrey. After her examination Geoffrey looked puzzled and could give no positive explanation and advised that we monitor the situation. The one thing that was possible was that she had maybe knocked her head at some point and was little concussed. It wasn't until we arrived home that I remembered something that had happened in the garden a few days previous. One of my little games with Laurel consisted of me sitting on the grass, throwing her ball up in the air and then punching it away from me for her to go and retrieve. This time I threw the ball in the air and just as I brought my fist up, Laurel jumped toward the ball. I caught Laurel square under her chin with a right uppercut Muhammad Ali would have been proud of. With my hand throbbing, Laurel looked at me, shook

her head and ran after the ball obviously with no ill effect. This was probably what caused her eye problem. Luckily she had no ill effects after a few days but it did cause a few laughs when I relayed the story to friends.

One thing Laurel loved playing with outside was a tennis ball. She would, if allowed run backwards and forwards with a ball for hours on end. With her development of arthritis, however, this had to be dramatically reduced. I limited this to the back garden for short periods of time. Over the next few months her legs didn't appear to worsen

169

but didn't appear to improve either so it really was 'fingers crossed'. After one particular day in the back garden something happened that made me realise I would have to confiscate Laurel's tennis ball for good. It wasn't the shear physical exercise with the ball that seemed to cause Laurel any problems but I began to notice how she twisted to retrieve the ball. After me throwing the ball a short distance she would go hell for leather to retrieve it. As she built up speed, nine times out of ten she would 'over shoot' the ball so have to turn quickly to get back to it. It was this action that was causing her legs some problems and on a couple of occasions she returned with the ball limping slightly. It didn't matter how far or how near the ball was thrown, this would nearly always happen. On this particular day she ran for the ball, missed it so had to turn quickly and obviously twisted her legs. She went down with a yelp. In the six years I had been with Laurel I could never remember her yelping the way she did that day. I ran to her, by which time she was on her feet limping badly. She left her ball where it was and moved to the shade to lay down. I'd seen enough – no more Tennis balls. That evening she gave out the same yelp when she got onto her chair so I knew the pain must have been bad. With plenty of rest Laurel was fine again within a couple of days and when going into the back garden she will still – even to this day – go to the garage where I kept her tennis balls. It makes me feel a little guilty but I know Laurel's health can only benefit from it

Greying a little aren't we?

CHAPTER TWENTY-FOUR

"DEVIL DOG SAVAGES CHILD."

How often do we read these types of headlines in the press? They are nearly always accompanied by the only picture I think the press have of a Staffordshire bull terrier baring it's teeth and saliva running from its mouth. Then we read on to find out what really happened.

On this particular occasion an incident was reported in our local Evening News in which a small dog had been attacked by a Staffie and severely injured in a Norwich street. My first reaction was "What the bloody hell was the dog doing off its lead in a street and why didn't the 'owner' have it under control?" After reading this particular article I really felt for the poor young man who had seen his beloved pet attacked and also my thoughts were with the poor little dog but my anger was for the 'owner' of the Staffie. I also realised this would now encourage an influx of "savage" dog scares around Norfolk in the same way it does with the national press should a story like this one come to light. Sure enough they were to follow thick and fast with out cries off " All bull terriers should be put down". One particular incident reported prompted me to write a letter to the Eastern Evening News. The story in question ran with the headline " CHILD IN SAVAGE DOG SCARE". It went on to tell the story of how a young mother and her daughter were outside their home when a Staffie approached the little girl. The mother went on to say that the dog approached her daughter wagging it's tail and showing no aggression toward the little girl at all but to be on the safe side she picked up her daughter to which time the dog wagged it's tail even more and was off with it's 'owner'. Once again not under it's 'owners' full control. What follows is the letter I wrote to the Evening News after reading the article and to give the newspaper some credit it was published as the "star" letter for that evening.

NOT ALL STAFFIES ARE
SAVAGE DOGS.

After reading your recent articles concerning Staffordshire bull terriers, I felt it necessary to put pen to put pen to paper on the subject.

Not all Staffies are savage dogs! I've 'owned' a Staffie for six years and I can honestly say I've never had a more loyal friend in my life.

She absolutely adores people, especially children (they are known as the 'nanny' dog for that reason) and has never shown any aggression towards them whatsoever.

It is a known fact that Staffies are not too keen on other dogs, but mine will never chase another dog looking for a fight. It has even been known for her to be chased away by a cat! I know many people who own Staffiies and all say the same, that they are truly lovely pets and companions. In fact my local vet says that in his twenty-five years experience he has never come across a Staffie that has worried him.

I am beginning to wonder if the Evening News is beginning to sensationalise stories like other tabloid press.

Why was it necessary to print the story of the young toddler who had a Staffie jump up her under the heading

174

"Savage Dog Scare?" As the mother said it showed no sign of aggression. I totally agree with her when she immediately picked up her child because, as she said you cannot be too careful.

My heart goes out to the young man that had his dog attacked by a Staffie and being a great animal lover I do feel for the poor dog but I do firmly believe the blame lies with the 'owner' of the Staffie.

The first word I taught my dog was "leave" and now whoever gives that command to her, her jaws will open evey time. I do feel its time people stopped thinking that Staffies are the 'macho' dog to own.

Come on Evening News, give Staffies a break. They are no worse than any other breed of dog and much better than most.

STEPHEN MOORE.

Surprisingly this letter did not receive a response. I was expecting the anti – bull terrier brigade to jump on it but maybe it smacked of the truth.

At about the same time The Sun was running a big spread on the evil 'Devil Dogs' as they were called. This sparked a massive response from Staffie owners form all over the country (including myself) basically stating the same thing. The 'owners are to blame, not the dogs' The part of the e-mail I sent to The Sun (which they decided to publish) said everything. I wrote:

"I have owned a Staffie for six years and I can honestly say there is not a more loyal, loving and fun dog. As soon as my

175

dog sees a child her tail wags frantically and she lays on her back waiting for attention. Any dog can turn into a vicious creature with the wrong 'owner' – they are the ones to blame, not the dogs"

These stories all die down when they fail to sell newspapers and won't rear the head again until something else happens to grab the headlines. It is then we begin to have the so-called "attacks" daily again.

Recently Princess Anne's dog launched an attack on one of the Queen's beloved Corgis and again there were calls to have bull terriers banned. A few days later a maid was "savaged" by, supposedly, the same dog. While it is not a very nice incident I believe if the maid had been "savaged" she wouldn't be here to tell the tale so thanks again to the newspapers for drumming up fear in these lovely animals. Once again the 'owner' (in this case the Princess Royal) comes into question also. Why weren't the dogs under her control? Something, I fear, we will never know.

At the end of the day I feel it's a case of trusting and more so, knowing your dog that could prevent these "attacks". Although I trust Laurel 100% I would never put her in a situation that would test that trust to the limit – it's just not fair on her. I have heard on many occasions, people saying, " Any dog can turn and attack" and to a certain extent that is true because I cannot, hand on heart, say that Laurel would not attack a person that was attacking me or if she was pushed into a corner that she had no way out of. I do know one thing – it would have to be a damn good reason for her to even contemplate such actions and of that I am more than certain!

True friends
Just as this photograph was taken Laurel decided to lick my
ear.

CHAPTER TWENTY-FIVE

THE PRESENT DAY.

About A year ago I carried out something that I know some people would find a little strange or at worst, morbid. I made two little coffins for Laurel and Harriet. This was my thinking behind my actions.

Many years ago when I was a teenager and Christine and I were together the first time around, she and her family had a little Westie called Cindy. Sadly on Boxing Day one year, little Cindy died and it was left to John to sort out the burial in the garden. Watching John making the coffin for Cindy was heartbreaking enough for me but I can't begin to think how he must have felt knowing his pet was going into the finished product and be gone forever. With these thoughts in my mind I decided to make the coffins for my two best mates while they were still around because I didn't think I would be capable when the sad day came. I spent a day in the summer making two lovely wooden boxes with the care and love that both Laurel and Harri deserve and although it did upset me making them I knew that at anytime I could leave the garage and go outside to play with both Laurel or Harri. Not the situation John was in. I feel sure Laurel must have wondered what was going on as she saw me disappear into the garage only to reappear after much sawing and banging with tears in my eyes. Once they were both made I placed several white sheets in both coffins and stored them out of sight in the garage where I hope they will remain for many years to

179

come. I've cared for them both to the best of my ability while they are both alive so I felt this would be my final act of kindness to them when they leave me. Until now Christine is the only other person that knew of my actions and of course, Christine being Christine was full of support and understanding.

As I write it is now early January 2004 and both Laurel and Harri are well, which is a little more than can be said for Rosie. Rosie is still living with Christine's parents and has terrible breathing problems that cannot be cured, only controlled. The poor little mite is such a happy little thing but is constantly gasping for breath. It is also thought she has an enlarged heart which doesn't bode well. With the constant stream of steroids she needs to take, her weight has increased so coupled with the breathing problems, she struggles a little to get around but is still wonderfully happy. She rarely fails to greet anyone that enters her home with the tail wag and lick of the nose but once the greeting is finished she's off to find a nice cool spot to lie down and rest – until any form of food appears that is. She still has that little sparkle in her eye. As with Laurel, we all know the problem is not going away but making life as comfortable as possible is top priority and just like me, with Laurel, Doreen is doing everything she can to achieve this for Rosie.

Harri, now at the ripe old age of twelve, spends a great deal of time on top of the boiler in our utility room. It's funny how animals have that knack of finding the warmest place in the house isn't it? She still looks the same as she did ten years ago and only recently had to have her teeth de-scaled at the vets for the first time. Not bad for an aging cat. As I have always said about Harri – she is always there. She rarely fails to come out to greet me when I arrive home – in the summer months anyway. It's far too cold to venture from her prime spot in the winter months and who can blame her? She really is a lovely cat.

As for my Laurel – as mad as ever is the expression I would have to use. I have to say in the past month or so her rear legs are the best I have seen them since she was diagnosed a year ago. With her weight monitored, her exercise restricted and her daily medication she seems fine. I realise this terrible debilitating disease has not gone away and could cripple her at any moment and I still occasionally notice her lifting her legs off the floor, obviously to relieve pain but at present she is fairing well.

On one occasion during the year when we were on holiday my parents had to take Laurel to see Geoffrey for a check-up on her legs and whilst waiting to be called in, decided to check Laurel's weight on the scales provided. Because of Laurel's excitement at being in the vets surgery there was no way she would stand still long enough for Mum to see her weight. That's when a very nice girl on reception, seeing the problems they were having, decided to intervene and help. Not a good move as this excited Laurel even more. " I think it would be easier if I weighed myself, then picked up Laurel and weighed us both together" was the brilliant suggestion from the young girl. Brilliant if you're not dealing with Laurel that is. Of course when she picked Laurel off the floor she turned into a wiggly worm. Licking all over her face, chewing her hair the poor girl must have realised it was going to be impossible. As all of this was happening Geoffrey appeared from his room and upon seeing what was happening calmly said, " You have got no chance!" At which point the poor girl had to admit defeat. Laurel was eventually weighed in Geoffrey's surgery but this whole incident caused tremendous amusement and is still talked about today. I just hope it wasn't the young girls first day at the clinic.

There was a little scare a few months ago when Laurel was having quite a lot of tummy problems. She wasn't herself at all and seemed very depressed most of the time. Very unusual for Laurel. This was quickly diagnosed as acute colitis and was treated by spreading feeding times and the type of food she was taking. I did have a real shock when for the first time Geoffrey was talking of tumours and the dreaded 'C' word when I described her symptoms but luckily it was nothing more serious than a bout of colitis.

She still goes crazy at the word "bucket" and has just begun the same response to another word. That word being "guitar". I have had an acoustic guitar standing in our lounge since we moved into the property some two years ago and Laurel has just taken notice of it. If any mention of the word "guitar" is uttered she goes straight over to it and barks her mad little head off. I think only she will ever know the reason why. Maybe it's my playing, who knows? She is also still very wary when people raise their voices even if it is just a simple heated debate. This sometimes sparks off the tail chasing, which has not completely stopped and I put this firmly down to the ' Debbie' days. When Christine and me are clowning around play –

fighting, Laurel is up immediately and literally gets in between the two of us until we stop. I know some of this behaviour can be put down to Laurel being slightly jealous when other people are with me and this stems from all the time her and I spent on our own but I think a lot of the behaviour goes deeper than that. On some occasions she will lie in her bed and just stare at me for hours almost as if she thinks I going somewhere. On my night shifts she is absolutely fine with Christine and Emma and it's great for me to know she is left in more than capable hands while I am at work.

I feel very lucky in meeting Christine again after many years apart and I know her and Laurel are very close. Emma does care for Laurel but to her I think Laurel is just a dog. When we are all in the house together Laurel will often disappear only to be found lying behind Christine in the bathroom almost as if she is guarding her. She has also been found on occasions lying in Emma's bedroom while Emma is sleeping. I think it's safe to say we are all very, very happy.

Since Laurel arrived on the scene some seven years ago now, she has made me very happy and I would even go so far as to say it's difficult not to be happy when she is around. She has the wonderful knack of making people smile. She has helped me through sad times and the help she has given to my parent's well being is irreplaceable. She really is a truly remarkable companion.

AUTHOR'S COMMENTS.

THE CORRECT DECISION?

Going back to the beginning of this book when it was decision time for me on whether to go for having a dog or not, I often mull over the comments that were given to me on the issue.

"It'll ruin your house". The only thing I can ever remember Laurel 'wrecking' were the curtains in her bedding area when we lived in Old Catton and to be honest that episode made me laugh more than anything. She has never chewed furniture, shoes, clothes or the like mainly because at a young age she was never given the opportunity to.

"They are a terrible tie". I slightly agree with this one but again at a very young age she was used to being left for short periods of time and still, to this day is no problem at all when being left on her own. With the added bonus of her being able to go to my parents at holiday times (for which I am forever grateful to them for) Laurel is not really a tie at all – only when I want her to be.

"Staffies are a vicious breed of dog". I think enough has been said in this book to show that Laurel could never be mentioned in the same sentence as the word vicious. As for her and Harriet getting along together – they are best buddies. If anyone ever asks how to two react to each other I simply say "No problems – and anyway it'd be hard for

185

Laurel to attack Harri when she's running in the opposite direction from her!"

I have left one of the original statements out because I have to say I do totally agree with it. There is one area that Laurel will let me down because nature won't allow her to do anything else. I know one day she will break my heart.
Did I make the correct decision? What do you think?

ISBN 141202621-0

4170187R00105

Printed in Great Britain
by Amazon.co.uk, Ltd.,
Marston Gate.